Stress proof
your business
and your life

By Steve Pipe and Elisabeth Wilson

infiniteideas

This book is dedicated with love and thanks to Mum and Dad.

Copyright © Steve Pipe and Infinite Ideas, 2010
The right of Steve Pipe and Elisabeth Wilson to be identified as the authors of this book has been asserted in accordance with the Copyright, Designs and Patents Act 1988.

First published in 2010 by
Infinite Ideas Limited
36 St Giles
Oxford
OX1 3LD
United Kingdom
www.infideas.com

A CIP catalogue record for this book is available from the British Library

ISBN 978–1–906821–61–6

Brand and product names are trademarks or registered trademarks of their respective owners.

Designed and typeset by Nicki Averill
Printed and bound by Ashford Colour Press Ltd, Gosport, Hampshire

Contents

Part 3: Stress proofing the personal stuff   **91**

Part 4: Making it all happen   **147**

Introduction

Let's face it, life is stressful.

When you own and run a business, those stresses tend to be magnified. A recent survey suggests that they are being magnified further as the economic situation deteriorates. So in this book we are looking specifically at what you as a business leader can do to reduce your stress levels.

Part 1, Stress proofing the business stuff, looks at what you can do to reduce and prevent the stress caused by your business and its financial situation. In Part 2, Stress proofing the money stuff, we look at what you can do to reduce and prevent the stress caused by your personal financial situation. In these first two parts much of the emphasis is on strengthening the financial and business fundamentals – since they are so often the primary sources of stress and anxiety for business leaders. So addressing them is often by far the best way of eliminating stress.

Part 3, Stress proofing the personal stuff, broadens the discussion by explaining how to reduce and prevent the stress caused by the other things going on in your life. It also gives you practical strategies for dealing with the stresses in your life, no matter how they are caused. Finally, Part 4 brings it all together into a practical action plan that shows you how to take the ideas in these pages and use them to improve your life.

Because we know that your time is precious we have been very, very selective. We have only included things that will make a profound difference, things that are practical, things that are specifically relevant to you as a business leader. These are the things that we regard as the 44 Keys to stress reduction that will help you to reduce stress from the moment you start using them.

Everything in these pages has been proven to work, and will work for you too.

Part 1
Stress proofing the business stuff

Introduction

Owning and running a business can be incredibly stressful. The main causes of this business related stress include:

- Not making enough profit
- Running out of cash and other similar cashflow problems
- Being forced to work more than you want to
- Having too many things on your to-do list
- Too much depending on you, and too many things that can only be done by you
- Not getting the right life–work balance
- Not having the information you need to make sensible decisions
- Losing too much of what you earn to the taxman
- Having the wrong kind of customers
- Other people, especially customers and your employees, behaving unreasonably or unfairly
- Having your hard earned money stolen from you
- Letting customers down by making mistakes

In this section you will discover how to make all of these problems a distant memory.

Key 1
Systems are the solution to a better business and an easier life

There is a key difference between having a job and owning a business: a job requires you to do the work personally, while a business does not. The sad reality for many small business owners is that, in practice, they don't actually have a business, they have a job. Worse still, they are employed by a slave driver (themselves). And as a result they end up putting in more and more hours, and becoming more and more stressed.

But while the business owner keeps running out of hours in the day, their employees are often running out of things to do, because much of what needs doing can only be done by the owner. As a result the lament, "If only my employees could do things as well as I do, we wouldn't have a problem," can be heard through the clenched teeth of just about every business owner in the country.

Happily that lament also contains the solution. All business owners need to do is turn it into the question:

> *What do I need to do so that others in the business can do everything in the same way and to the same standard that I would do it myself?*

And then the answer becomes obvious. You need to write down everything you do and exactly how you do it in the form of a set of detailed step by step instructions. These instructions then become the systems on which the business is based.

Your systems can take many forms (procedures manuals, written scripts, standard forms, checklists, etc.) but once they have been created, they can be used to train and guide other people in the business to do the things that previously only the business owner could do. So you no longer have to do any of those things personally and you get your life back.

I have seen hundreds of business owners benefit from exactly this approach. I have also applied it in my own twenty-five person business with great effect (so much so that, at the age of forty-eight, I was able to switch to a ninety day a year working arrangement).

Of course, I am not suggesting that systemising your business is an overnight job. For example, we have been systemising our business for over ten years, and there is still more to be done. It is hard work, and it takes time. But, on a personal level alone, the rewards fully justify the effort and are genuinely life changing. You will be in control of your life. You will be able to choose how many hours to work, and how to spend those hours. And you will be able to spend more time on the other things that are important to you too, such as your family, health and hobbies.

The benefits of systems

As well as having personal benefits, systemising your business in this way will also make your business much more successful. For example, the benefits of having systems include:

- They allow you to step back from working IN the business and concentrate on working ON the business.
- The business is less dependent on any individual or group – because anyone can run the system. So you'll never need to fear staff illnesses, retirements, defections or industrial disputes again.
- The business is easier to grow since its success can be replicated by others using the systems.
- The systems can be tested and improved in a systematic and scientific way. As a result, everyone ends up using the same optimal processes – rather than doing things in their own (often sub-optimal) way.
- What you do, how you do it and the results you get all become more consistent and predictable.
- So, for all these reasons, the business becomes more valuable and saleable – and probably more profitable too.

These are just a few of the reasons why systems are so powerful. It is therefore perhaps not surprising that many people claim that the word SYSTEM actually stands for Save Your Self Time, Earn yourself Money.

Just imagine how much less stressed you will be when the business does not depend on you. When you know that everything is being done to the same high standard you would do it yourself. When the business results are predictably better. And when you are in complete control of your life–work balance because you are able to choose how much or how little work you personally do.

Key 2
Achieve more with less effort

As business owners, we work hard, we worry, and we get stressed. So here's a liberating truth: only a few things are really important, most things are not.

Of course, that statement is true on many different spiritual and philosophical levels. And any one of those may help you to keep your business related issues in perspective. But I want you to be liberated by looking at it from a purely commercial perspective, and to do that I want to remind you of the 80/20 principle.

The 80/20 principle says that the minority (20%, say) of causes, inputs or efforts usually lead to a majority (80%, say) of the results, outputs or rewards. This means that, for example, 80% of what you achieve comes from 20% of the time spent. So for all practical purposes, 80% of the effort – a dominant part of it – is largely irrelevant.

In other words, a few things are important, but most things are not.

The important few often represent around 20%. But there is nothing magical about that exact percentage – it could be 10% or 30%. The key is that there is an imbalance, with some things being far more important than others.

Examples include:

- Roughly 20% of customers, markets and services generate roughly 80% of profits;

- Roughly 20% of the things on your to-do list will generate roughly 80% of your results;
- Roughly 20% of your decisions will lead to roughly 80% of your progress.

Conventional wisdom is not to put all your eggs into one basket. But 80/20 wisdom is to choose your basket very carefully (i.e. so that it reflects the important 20%), put all your eggs in it and then watch it like a hawk. This approach will generate the most money with the least expenditure of assets and effort.

This is made possible by:

- Accurately identifying the important 20% – and doing much more of it;
- Identifying the unimportant 80% – and either making it much more effective or doing much less of it.

Example

To keep the maths simple, imagine a situation where 100 hours of your effort generates £10,000 of income. The 80/20 principle suggests that the most important 20 of those hours will generate £8,000 of income – with the other 80 hours generating just £2,000. So if you reorganised your business so that you cut out the less important 80 hours, and if you used 20 of those 80 hours saved to replicate your most important 20 hours (i.e. do two lots of the most important 20 hours) you would generate another £8,000 of income. The net result would be that you would earn £16,000 for 40 hours work. **This represents a 60% reduction in your workload and a 60% increase in your total income.** Or, looking at it another way, a 400% increase in hourly income.

Clearly the maths in this example has been simplified, and many other permutations are possible. But in each case the conclusion is the same. The 80/20 principle helps you to make more money with less effort.

How to start applying 80/20 to your business

The ideal place to start is to work with your accountant to identify:

- The 20% of your customers that generate 80% of your profits;
- The 20% of your products and services that generate 80% of your profits;
- The 20% of markets that generate 80% of your profits;
- The 20% of distribution channels that generate 80% of your profits.

Then explore in detail what you can do to get more of your 20% customers, sell more of your 20% products and services, and penetrate more fully your 20% markets and channels.

Also explore how you can make your 80% customers, products, services, markets and channels more profitable. And if that isn't possible, consider scaling down or even withdrawing from those areas.

Remember, though, that there is nothing magical about the numbers being exactly 20% and 80%. You are simply looking for an imbalance between what you put in and what you get out.

It applies to your life!

Also remember that the 80/20 principle doesn't just apply to your business. It applies to every other aspect of your life too. As Richard Koch says:

You can take your own small fragments of greatest achievement, happiness and service to others and make them a much larger part of your life. You can multiply your highs and cut out most of your lows. You can identify the mass of irrelevant and low value activity and begin to shed this worthless skin. You can become a better, more useful and happier human being. And you can help others to do the same.

Key 3
Taming your to-do list

As a business owner myself, one of the main causes of stress for me used to be the sense of foreboding I got from having a to-do list that seemed to stretch from here to eternity. But all that changed when I started to use a simple spreadsheet to arrange my to-do list differently.

Simple as the spreadsheet system is, I can honestly say that it has transformed my productivity and my working life. For example, the benefits to me personally of using it include:

1. It makes sure I do the stuff that is urgent;
2. It prevents me overlooking the stuff that is important but not necessarily urgent;
3. It means I can literally forget about the things that simply don't need to be dealt with at the moment – secure in the knowledge that they will automatically resurface when their time comes;
4. And it allows me to feel fully in control.

I can't tell you how much less stressful this all is, and as a result how much more productive I am, than when I used to keep a seemingly endless to-do list with every outstanding action on it.

How the to-do list spreadsheet works

- The spreadsheet contains separate worksheets for each of my main areas of responsibility – for example, research, writing and seminars. Whenever I identify a new action point I immediately add it to the relevant worksheet, and assign a do-by date to it.

■ I also record business improvement ideas in exactly the same way – except instead of assigning a date, I simply write 'Idea' in the date column so that I know this is merely something to consider in due course rather than something that must be acted on by a certain date.

■ Every few days I re-sort each of the worksheets in date order, and transfer the things that need doing that week to a separate to-do list worksheet, which I print out on one side of a sheet of A4.

■ I keep the resulting printed to-do list on the top of my desk, and manually colour in each action on it with a yellow highlighter pen as I complete it to give me a visible way of tracking progress.

■ My current actions are printed on the left hand side of my A4 to-do list page, leaving the right hand side of the page free for something equally important … whenever I am waiting for someone else to get back to me or do something before I can take my next step, I list that in pen in a column on the right, and yellow highlight it once they have done their part and the ball is back in my court. This way I can see at a glance what is outstanding, and I can easily chase when needed.

As a result I always know what to focus my energies on at any point in time, and what I am waiting on others for. I also know that all my future actions are logged and are in hand, and because my resulting printed to-do list is always quite short, it always seems manageable.

And I get real pleasure from seeing what I have already achieved, as evidenced by all the yellow highlights.

In addition, because my non-current actions are carefully recorded out of sight on a spreadsheet they are fully under control, but they never prey on my mind. So I never feel swamped by them, as I used to when they all appeared on a single action plan document that stretched for pages.

To me the psychological impact of these benefits is priceless. They completely remove the stress and anxiety I used to feel, and ensure that I always feel in control.

They will do the same for you.

Key 4
Preventing your team delegating work up to you

Your employees are supposed to make your life easier. All too often, though, they end up making your life harder as your time is spent solving problems brought to you by your team.

Imagine the scene: a team member comes up to you and says "We have a problem"... they then spend fifteen minutes telling you about it ... and you end up saying "Leave it with me and I'll see what I can do." As a result their problem becomes your problem. And you end up doing everybody else's work.

Sound familiar?!

Blanchard and Oncken describe this as 'Letting a monkey jump from their back onto yours' – and they argue that it is one of the biggest thieves of a business leader's time. The monkey is the next step – and the key to effective delegation is only agreeing to take the next step yourself (i.e. to let the monkey jump onto your back) if it is a step that ONLY you can take.

The six step solution

More specifically, the monkey management approach is as follows:

Step 1

When a member of your team brings you a problem say: "We both need to understand that we don't have problems. If there is a problem it is either yours or mine. And if it is your problem I will help you with it on the clear understanding that it will never become my problem. So at the end of this meeting it will be you that has to do whatever it is that we agree needs doing. Does that make sense?"

And also make it clear in advance that whenever a team member brings a problem to you they must also bring at least one suggestion for the next step. (This requirement alone will greatly reduce the number of problems brought to you – since in thinking of their suggested next steps your staff will often discover that they can solve the whole thing without involving you!)

Step 2

As they tell you about the problem and their suggested next steps, decide what needs to happen next – which could be to go with one of their suggestions, do something else you dreamed up at the meeting, or go away and research some other solutions.

Step 3

Agree who is to take that next step or steps. (Remember, this next step is the 'monkey' – and you should only let it jump on your back if it is a step that only you can take!)

Step 4

Agree whether they have full authority to take the next steps and then report back to you – or whether they need to come back to you with more recommendations before they can take some or all of the next steps – which should only be necessary where the problem is either very important or you have serious doubts that the person is fully up to the task.

Step 5
Agree a time when they will report back to you.

Step 6
At that next meeting go back to Step 1 and start again. Continue looping through the six step process in this way until the problem has been solved.

This simple six step process will prevent your team delegating work up to you. While systemising your business, as discussed earlier in Key 1, will mean you can delegate as much as you want down to them.

Together these two processes will ensure that you will never again end up doing everything.

Key 5
The three essential frames of reference for understanding and improving your results and profits

Would your life be less stressful if your profits were much higher?

The answer is almost certainly yes, isn't it? After all, higher profits would give you more breathing space and more security. Higher profits would also give you more options. For example you would be able to afford to:

- Get rid of customers who cause you grief;
- Improve your technology, systems and team so that the business runs more smoothly;
- Employ someone to do some or all of your job, so that you get a better life–work balance.

We will look at how you can improve your profits in the pages that follow. But first it is important to recognise that in order to IMPROVE profitability, you first need to fully UNDERSTAND your profitability. Unfortunately, a traditional set of accounts doesn't really help anyone to properly understand the profitability of a business. For example, if a business has profits of £50,000, is that good or bad?

The answer is: it depends. More specifically, it depends on three crucially important frames of reference: what the business has achieved in the past, what you hoped to achieve this time, and what others in the same industry are achieving.

Frame of reference 1 - your past

To continue our example, if a business had earned £700,000 in each of the last three years, then you would probably regard this year's £50,000 profits as bad. On the other hand, had it only earned £300 profits in the past, you would probably regard this year's £50,000 as good.

Frame of reference 2 - your plans

If you had planned to make £700,000 you would probably regard this year's £50,000 as bad. But if you had only planned to make £300 you would no doubt regard this year's £50,000 as good.

Frame of reference 3 - your industry

If everyone else in the industry was making profits of £700,000 you would probably judge £50,000 to be bad. Whereas you would judge it as good if everyone else was only earning profits of £300.

These three frames of reference are equally applicable to all the other key performance measures in your business, including gross margins, debtor days and growth rates. Before you can start to create a plan to improve your performance – including your profitability – you need to fully understand your performance across these three essential frames of reference.

And that means that, at the very least, you need:

1. Trend reports – showing graphically how the performance of your business has varied over the last three to five years.
2. Variance reports – revealing how your performance compares to your forecasts, budgets and plans.
3. Benchmarking reports – showing how your performance compares to the rest of your industry.

Together this information will help you to understand your strengths and weaknesses, spot patterns and trends, see where things are getting better or worse, identify things you used to do in the past that would help you to get better results if you started doing them again, see what else is possible, work out where to focus your efforts and energies, and create an improvement plan.

If you do not have all of this information at your fingertips – or if it is not up to date, accurate and in a readily accessible format – ask your accountant to help you get it as a matter of urgency.

Which of the three reports is most important?

While all three of these frames of reference and reports are vitally important, I will get off the fence and tell you which I regard as the most important. If I could only produce one of the three reports for a business, it would always be a benchmarking report. No question.

Why? Because most business owners already have some kind of sense of how they are doing compared to their plans and past performance. But I rarely meet a business owner that has an accurate idea of how they are doing compared to the rest of their industry. Yes, they have a view on it. But that view is usually based on guesswork rather than fact. And in most cases it is so wide of the mark as to be positively harmful.

I have lost count of the number of times entrepreneurs have said to me, "You don't understand my industry. It is impossible to earn more than X per cent margin, or get paid in less than Y days. That's just the way it is."

The only effective way to deal with those limiting beliefs is to go off and get the facts. Which means benchmarking them. Occasionally the evidence from benchmarking confirms their beliefs. But usually it shows that they were wrong and that some others in their industry are getting much better results than they thought were possible.

And where that is the case, the business owners are usually transformed. Gone is the very stressful 'there's nothing we can do' victim mindset, instead they are so much more positive. They realise that they don't have to settle for their current results. They realise it is not a question of IF they can improve things. It is a question of HOW they can improve things. And they are energised in their quest to find the HOW (which is also the quest that we will be turning our attention to next in this book).

A word of warning

Whatever you do, never ever use industry averages from Companies House to benchmark your business.

No matter how careful you are with Companies House data, it always suffers from one fundamental flaw: most businesses do not put the right SIC code on their annual return.

So if you use Companies House SIC averages you will, in all probability, be making meaningless and misleading comparisons against a random collection of businesses that bear no relation to yours.

Key 6
Everything you need on
a single page

Some businesses produce a mind boggling amount of performance data and financial information. While other businesses produce almost no up to date and useful numbers at all.

Either way it's a recipe for stress. Too much and the owners feel like they are swamped and overwhelmed. Too little and they have no real idea of what is going on. The key is to get the balance right so that you have your finger on the pulse of everything that matters in your business, presented in a format that can be instantly understood and acted upon by all the decision makers in your business.

Achieve that and you will not only greatly reduce your stress, and the stress levels of your team, but you will also start making better decisions and getting better results.

Why management accounts are not enough

Traditionally, most business information systems consist of a set of detailed management accounts, i.e. monthly profit and loss accounts, balance sheet and cashflow. But most successful businesses recognise that traditional management accounts do not give them anywhere near enough information to really drive their businesses forward. So they also measure other Key Success Drivers (also known as Key Performance Indicators or KPIs), so that they can really understand what is happening while there is still time to do something about it.

For example, the only information traditional management accounts give about sales is the value of invoices raised. But for many businesses that kind of backwards looking lag indicator is not very useful for understanding what is already happening, or predicting what will happen next. Much more helpful for managing sales are Key Success Drivers such as the number of sales leads, the conversion rate from lead to sale and the size of the order book.

So most successful businesses now systematically map out and measure those kinds of Key Success Drivers too. In fact, the most successful businesses now systematically identify and measure Key Success Drivers for every key area of their business.

More can be less

But how can you ensure this Key Success Driver approach doesn't just add to your information overload? And how does it simplify matters?

The answer lies in creating a One Page Plan – which, as its name suggests, distils all the key numbers onto a single sheet of A4. And One Page Plans are normally structured like this:

■ The One Page Plan starts at the bottom of the page and works upwards. So it starts with the business's mission/ vision/goals.

- Those goals, in turn, determine the key areas in which the business will have to excel in order to achieve its goals (i.e. the Underlying Success Drivers).

- Next come the key factors that directly drive the business's sales, costs and cashflow (which are so important that they are each given their own section of the page).

- Some of these numbers come from the management accounts – but many of them do not.

- Wherever possible they are lead indicators in that they help you understand what is going to happen in the future, i.e. just as the size of the order book helps you to understand and predict future sales. But in some cases they are unavoidably lag indicators, merely telling you what has happened already.

- And finally there are the key results that have been generated by all the underlying drivers. These key results are, of course, lag indicators. And they are deliberately positioned at the top of the page because they are the consequence of everything below them on the page.

In this way the One Page Plan describes all the key factors behind a business's success, and maps them out in a logical way that mirrors the causal links between goals, success drivers and eventual results. Not only does this give you an early warning system by systematically measuring and monitoring everything that is really important in the business, but it also acts as a catalyst for identifying the action that needs to be taken, and as a mechanism for recording and monitoring your constantly updated action plan.

Example Company - July 2010
The latest update to our *OnePage*™ business plan for the year ended 30 July 2010

Key results	Actual	Target	Comments
Value of business	**£3.3m**	£6.0m	We are on track to be worth £6 million by 31/12/15 – well done.
Profit	**£76,235**	£67,000	Again, excellent. Thank you everyone. Keep up the great work!
Cash	**£36,334**	£50,000	We must tighten our credit control procedures up (see below)

Key sales drivers	Actual Target	Key actions	Key cost & cash drivers		Key actions
Number of referrals received	**105** 90	Great work. Keep it up!	Cost per unit	**£166** £150	Change supplier Negotiation training
Number of other sales enquiries generated	**200** 250	3D marketing Launch web-site	Mailshot costs per thousand	**£675** £585	Switch to Mailsort
Conversion rate from enquiry to customer	**62%** 60%	Produce audio tape answering FAQs	Debtor days	**17** 15	Tighten credit control. Review procedures and use new debt collection letter
Proportion of customers who have bought 3 times in last 12 months	**91%** 95%	Launch loyalty programme			
Average spend per customer pa	**£1560** £1750	Test new cross selling system.			
Market share	**25%** 23%	Competitor analysis			

Key underlying success drivers		Actual Target		Key actions
Customer delight	Average customer satisfaction feedback scores out of 5	**4.3** 4.5		Conduct in depth interview with 10 customers to identify how to make them even happier
Team happiness	Weekly "happiness" scores from timesheet - out of 10	**8.9** 8.5		Organise bowling evening
Investment in our people	Time spent training - hours	**285** 275		Board to attend Tom Peters course
Innovation	New ideas generated and % implemented	**215** 150	**64 %** 67%	Organise innovation awayday
	Time spent on R&D for new products - hours	**475** 450		
	New products launched this year - YTD	**67** 70		Finish the three new products currently in the pipeline

Our Mission/Vision/Goals
We are building the world's leading widget manufacturing company. By the end of 2015 the business will have a 50% market share in the UK and be valued at £6 million pounds.

It could change your life

There are so many benefits from this approach, that it is not an exaggeration to say that it could change your business and your life.

1. Because a One Page Plan is so simple and readily understandable by everybody from the shop floor to the Board, it will have a profound effect on their willingness and ability to contribute to the business.

2. By sharing it with your team you instantly overcome the complaint: 'they never tell us anything.' As a result, they feel trusted, involved and empowered.

3. It tells them how they are doing, helps them to identify the areas they need to work on, and forces them to think about, record and monitor the action they are going to take to do even better in the future.

4. It can (and must) be updated easily and quickly on a monthly basis – making it a living document that always records the most up to date performance information and the most up to date action plans.

5. Forcing them to draw up a monthly action plan, helps them to actually take action … which, as you know, is ultimately the key to success (but is all too often overlooked because we are all too busy doing the things we have always done).

6. It can (and ideally should) be posted on notice boards, etc., so that everybody in the business knows exactly what the business is trying to achieve, how far they have got towards achieving it, and what they can do to get the business there even faster.

When used in this way it provides a focus for discussion, effort and creativity. It also acts as a brilliant tool to motivate your entire workforce – because one of the main reasons for demotivation is that they cannot see the point or the importance of what they or the business are doing and the One Page Plan makes all of that a thing of the past.

Proof

This is a true story. Five years ago a small scaffolding contracting business was turning over £100,000 and its owner was working ten to fifteen hour days. Since starting to use a One Page Plan every month their sales have grown to over £1 million and the owner now works four to six hours a day.

According to the owner, 90% of that improvement is down to the systematic and disciplined use of a One Page Plan in a way that has focussed their attention on the key issues and helped them to continuously fine-tune their action plan in order to make the business more and more successful.

The accountant in me says...

Wearing my hat as an accountant, I would regard the recommendation to use a One Page Plan to be one of the most important in the entire book. All good accountants can show you how to make this idea work for you. So what are you waiting for? Make a start today.

Key 7
The two types of money

Money is a major cause of stress. Or, to be more accurate, not having enough money is a major cause of stress. So let's take a fresh look at your options for getting more money.

Here's an indisputable truth: all the money you could possibly want already exists. It is just in somebody else's bank account. So your challenge is to get it from their bank account and into yours … legally, honestly, and with integrity.

And another indisputable truth: some money from some bank accounts you have to pay back, while some is non-repayable and you get to keep it forever.

Repayable money, for example a loan, has its place. But it comes at a price. So my guess is that you will sleep much more easily at night if your money is non-repayable, i.e. yours to keep forever and yours to spend in any way you want. So that's the type of money we are going to focus on here.

For most businesses there are two main sources of non-repayable money:

1. Customers – When you make sales, and get paid for them, the profits are yours to keep. So the first key is to make more profitable sales, and get paid for them more quickly.

2. The government – When you pay less tax, you keep more of your own money. So the second key is to reduce your tax

bills to the absolute legal minimum, and increase your tax refunds to the absolute legal maximum.

These two areas are mission critical to your business bank account, your personal bank account and to your life.

Your life depends on it

Your business is probably your main source of income and wealth. So most of what you want in life will ultimately have to be paid for from these two sources of non-repayable cash.

Your lifestyle (cars, holidays, luxuries and houses); the education, head-start and helping hand for getting on the housing ladder you are able to give to your children; the time out you need to follow your dreams and passions; and the joy and dignity in retirement, ill health and old age that you are able to ensure for your loved ones, as well as for yourself all depend on getting the best possible advice, and creating the best possible plan, to get the money you need from these two sources of non-repayable cash.

So I make no apology for the fact that the rest of Part 1 of this book explores in detail how you can:

- Get paid more quickly;
- Make more profitable sales;
- Pay no more than the legal minimum in tax.

After all, in a very real way, your life depends on it.

Key 8
Getting paid more quickly

Research and common sense tells us that being the victim of a crime is extremely stressful. So it is perhaps no wonder that most business owners are stressed, since they are regularly the victims of a particularly nasty type of crime. A crime committed on a daily basis by customers. The crime of not paying what they owe.

Surely that isn't really a crime, I hear you asking. Why not? After all, if someone walked out of a shop with a TV they hadn't paid for you would call that theft, wouldn't you? And it wouldn't cut any ice in the shop if they shouted back over their shoulder as they left: "I'll pay you next week." It is still wrong. Likewise, if a customer takes your product or service and never pays for it, they have in effect stolen from you.

Putting it bluntly, customers that never pay are thieves, pure and simple, while customers who don't pay on time are a serious threat to the survival of your business.

So your number one financial priority – now and on an ongoing basis – must be to ensure that your debt collection policies and systems are as good as humanly possible. And that means carrying out a detailed review of your credit control terms, policies and systems as a matter of urgency.

The benefits of ensuring this include:
- Improved cashflow through the faster collection of money owed;

- Less of your time and effort required to collect debts;
- Less money wasted on bad debts.

All of which will also lead to reduced costs, improved financial stability, fewer sleepless nights and less stress.

Essential first step

As I said earlier, I have lost count of the number of times business owners have said to me: "You don't understand my industry. It is impossible to get paid in less than X days. That's just the way it is." I have also lost track of the number of times that, when we went away and used benchmarking to see what others in the same industry were doing, we discovered that some were actually getting paid much more quickly.

What is really interesting, however, is that benchmarking evidence usually changed everything, since it motivated the owners to leave no stone unturned in their quest to match or beat those quicker collection speeds. It gave them an understanding of what was possible, and a target to aim for.

So the very first step you should take is to compare (i.e. benchmark) how quickly you get paid – your debtor days – against others in your industry.

However, please do remember that, as we saw earlier in Key 5, data from Companies House is likely to be completely misleading. So you will need to use a database that is not based on Companies House SIC code information. Of course, your accountant will be able to help you with this.

A practical idea to get you started

Some businesses have greatly reduced bad debts and collection costs, and completely eliminated all the delays and frustrations, by using direct debits and standing orders to get paid in full, on time, every time.

Standing order arrangements are usually very easy to set up. And they can be really helpful if you have customers who pay you the same amount on a regular basis (i.e. weekly, monthly, quarterly or even annually). However, they can be a hassle to change if, for example, your prices or the VAT rate changes.

Direct debits are far more flexible, since they allow you to take whatever amounts your customers owe you, direct from their bank accounts and on the day it is due. So they are often the ideal way to be paid. Until recently many banks made it difficult for smaller businesses to set up direct debit arrangements, but recent developments mean that direct debiting is now a feasible option for many more businesses. So if you haven't explored them in the last year or so, you should do so now.

Key 9
Making more profitable sales

As we saw earlier, making more profitable sales is crucial. We have already seen three ways to start approaching this challenge:

- Benchmarking – when you benchmark your gross margins against others in your industry you will begin to understand how much scope for improvement there really is.
- Product profitability analysis – which helps you to see which products/services are adding the most to your profits, and which are underperforming.
- Customer profitability analysis – which helps you to see which of your customers are most profitable, and to identify any that you are making hidden losses on.

In this section we are going to look at something which is arguably even more fundamentally important: the five sales drivers and three cost drivers that together constitute your eight profit drivers.

The five ways to increase sales: your sales drivers

There are only five ways to increase the sales of any business, including yours:

1. Getting more sales leads of the type you want.
2. Converting more of your sales leads into customers.

3. Increasing loyalty – improving customer retention, and reducing customer defection.
4. Increasing the average number of times your customers do business with you in a year, i.e. how many times they buy from you.
5. Increasing the average amount customers spend every time they do business with you, i.e. how much they buy from you. (One of the most important factors here is the way you price, which we will focus on in detail shortly.)

The three ways to reduce costs: your cost drivers

And there are only three ways to reduce costs in any business:

1. Improving productivity and efficiency so that you need fewer inputs (i.e. labour, materials, services, etc.) to support each £ of turnover.
2. Reducing the price you pay for inputs, including labour and raw material, i.e. by negotiating bigger discounts and lower wage rates, and switching to cheaper suppliers.
3. Managing your balance sheet better – so that balance sheet driven costs such as bad debts, funding and interest costs are reduced.

Your profit driver action plan

Together these five sales drivers and three cost drivers constitute the eight profit drivers for your business. And the key to improved profits it to create an action plan that focuses on these drivers.

So here are my six top tips for creating your profit driver action plan:

1. You can't cut your way to greatness. Working on the cost drivers tends to be slow and painful – after all, if cutting costs was quick and painless you would have done it already. It involves difficult decisions and stressful situations. Generally it also reduces the sum of human happiness and wealth (after all, if you pay a supplier less, they and their employees are less happy and less wealthy!).

2. Remember too that the scope for cost savings is finite, since the lowest you can theoretically reduce costs to is zero, whereas there is almost no limit to how far you can increase sales. So whilst your cost drivers are important, and should not be ignored, your sales drivers are far more important, and should be your main priority.

3. Start by considering your current action plan for each of the drivers. Do you have one? If not, your need is even more urgent! And if you do, how well is it working?

4. Then answer the question: what have we successfully done in the past that we no longer do enough of? So many businesses simply get out of the habit of doing things that work. For example, I regularly hear entrepreneurs say things like, "We used to get a lot of referrals when we asked for them, but I don't think we ask anymore."

5. Don't just focus on the obvious – which for most businesses is to do more advertising and other marketing to generate more sales leads. Look equally at the less obvious areas, such as how to improve your referral systems, sales meeting systems, follow-up systems, pricing systems, up-selling and

cross-selling systems, repeat business and customer loyalty systems.

6. Notice that the key word in the previous point is 'systems'. Don't leave your great ideas to chance. Instead build them into your systems so that they happen every time.

Key 10
Using prices to make your life better

There are two types of customers: the good and the bad.

Bad customers send your stress levels through the roof with their complaints, unreasonable demands and broken payment promises. Bad customers are also the ones that really care about your prices a lot – since they are the ones that choose you because you are cheap, and will leave you the instant someone else becomes cheaper.

But good customers – the honourable, decent, appreciative and profitable ones you want more of – care less about your prices. Obviously price still matters to them. But the value in what your products and services do for them is even more important.

So, instead of competing on price, you should compete on the basis of giving the right kind of customers maximum value rather than the lowest price.

What is 'maximum value'?

Essentially, 'value' is the gap between the benefits a customer perceives he is getting and the price he perceives he is paying. So offering 'maximum value' means offering a bigger gap than anyone else.

Competing on maximum value...

There are four keys to competing on maximum value:

1. Make sure that your products and services are exactly what your customers, especially your ideal customers, need and want, i.e. they offer the best and most appropriate combination of benefits.

2. Make sure that your customers fully understand those benefits – unless they understand that what you have to offer is special, they will assume it is average, and that means that you'll only be able to charge an average price. So managing their perceptions is vital.

3. Set your prices intelligently – having properly researched the facts and your options (we will look at this in a lot more detail in the next two sections).

4. Present, explain and defend your prices in the best possible way – using carefully chosen persuasive language in well designed marketing systems, sales systems and objection handling systems.

... and how it will reduce your stress levels

When you compete on maximum value several wonderful things happen.

You attract nicer people as customers. They are more appreciative of what you do. And they complain less often. So you get fewer hassles, and doing business with them is more pleasurable.

Which means it is far more emotionally rewarding. They have chosen you on value rather than low price, which means they will be more loyal and you won't lose them the moment a cheaper supplier comes along. They also pay you higher and more profitable prices, so it is far more financially rewarding for you too.

Which all adds up to less stress and more joy.

Key 11
Your magic price 1

Prices are the single most important element in your profit equation. Get them right and you make a profit. Get them wrong and you make a loss. If not corrected, those pricing induced losses lead to … cashflow meltdown, sleepless nights, redundancies and business failure. In a word, stress.

So to ensure your pricing does not cause you that kind of grief let's answer a couple of questions.

1. How much profit would you make by giving your products or services away for free? Well, your sales would be zero – so you wouldn't make a profit, would you?

2. How much profit would you make if you sold your product or services at, say, 1,000 times their current price? Well the

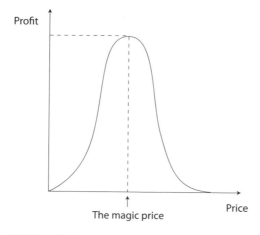

chances are that nobody would buy them. So again your sales would be zero – and again you wouldn't make a profit.

So at those two extremes – a ridiculously low price and a ridiculously high price – you don't make profits. But at some of the prices in between those two extremes you will make a profit. And at one price somewhere on that spectrum – we call it the MAGIC PRICE – you'll make the most profits.

And it is that magic price that you are looking for – the price that will earn you the most profits.

Have you got it right?

So here's the really important question for you … is the price you currently charge exactly that magic price? This is not a rhetorical question. I actually want you to say out loud one of two words: yes or no. Yes the price we charge is exactly the magic price. Or no, the price we charge isn't exactly the magic price.

So what's it going to be, yes or no?

If your answer was 'no', that's great – because it means that as you discover your magic price by working through the next few pages you will definitely be able to improve your profits, probably by a huge amount.

If your answer was 'yes' – how do you know that you are charging the magic price? How can you be sure, absolutely sure? What proof do you have? How strong and how up to date is your evidence? How many other prices have you tested? What is the precise impact on your short term and long term sales, and on your short term and long term profits, of your current price and all the other possible prices?

Finding your magic price

In one sense it is really easy. For every possible price, all you need to do is work out four things:

1. The quantity you will sell at that price;
2. The money value of those sales;
3. Your costs;
4. And, by deducting your costs from your sales, your profits.

Then you simply pick the price that gives you the highest profit. Simple?

In theory, yes, but not in practice. Once you know how many you are going to sell at each price, calculating your sales costs and profits should be fairly straightforward arithmetic. But the big problem, of course, is in estimating how many units you can sell at each price.

There are four ways to come up with such an estimate. The first three are:

1. Expert judgement;
2. Historical market data;
3. Customer surveys.

But they all have major weaknesses. There is probably nobody expert enough to give you reliable estimates – so usually it just ends up being guesswork. The historical market data you would need probably doesn't exist – and if it does it is probably out of date or relates to the prices of other companies' products, and isn't absolutely accurate (or perhaps even indeed relevant) for your situation today. And customer surveys sound like a good idea – but all too often customers say one thing in surveys and do something entirely different when it comes to actually parting with their hard earned cash.

The fourth method – testing

You may have to rely on those three methods to some extent. But wherever possible you should try to include at least some testing in your estimation process. After all, the only thing that really counts is not what experts think, or what happened in the past, or even what your customers say they will do. The only thing that matters is what happens when customers are asked to part with money. The only thing that actually matters is how much they actually spend at different prices. So you need to find ways of testing different prices.

But don't bet your business by doing anything reckless or irreversible. Be creative. And find ways to test different prices safely.

For example, you could change the price for a small group of customers – perhaps only through one of your distribution channels or shops. Or you could use a variety of different value coupons or discount vouchers to see how much you sell at different net prices. Or even use daily special offers to charge different prices on different days. The list of possibilities is enormous.

However you decide to test, always remember the two golden rules of testing:

1. Only change one thing at a time – since if you change more than one thing, for example the price and the packaging, you won't know whether it is the price change or the packaging change that causes customers to change how many they buy, will you?

2. Always measure the results before and after the change very carefully indeed.

And once you've found your magic price, make sure that is the price you actually charge.

Key 12
Your magic price 2: why a bottle of wine is the answer

In the previous section we looked at the importance of charging your magic price. But that is not the end of the story.

You see, your magic price isn't something handed down from on high – and neither are the profits you earn at that magic price. They are both something that you can actually choose. So changing your current price to something closer to your magic price is a great thing to do, and is also the easiest way to increase your profits since nothing else needs to change in your business. You get more profits without changing your product, service, marketing, packaging or overheads. Everything stays exactly the same except your prices and profits.

But you can make even more profit if you go one step further. And that further step is to consciously CHOOSE your magic price and the profits you earn at that magic price.

And to see what I mean by that I'd like to tell you a story about a bottle of wine.

The wrong thing to do with a bottle of wine

I'm looking at a bottle of Chardonnay. It has an unremarkable label, a non-existent vintage, and it is imported by a business in Luton that I have never heard of.

Now, what I'd like you to do is think about how much this bottle is going to sell for.

Retailer 1
Imagine that it is standing on the shelf in Sainsbury's. How much do you expect that bottle to be? Say a figure out loud.

Retailer 2
Now imagine a corner store. You know the kind of place. Run by a family who never seem to need any sleep, where the aunty and uncle, children and mum and dad work around the clock. And where everything is crammed in and stacked a little haphazardly.

Imagine that you spot the same bottle of Chardonnay amidst all that chaos. It is standing on the floor and there are six or seven bottles unattractively piled next to it. How much is that bottle of Chardonnay in that corner store? Say a figure out loud.

Retailer 3
Now imagine that you are in an independent wine merchant's and there on the shelf is this same bottle of Chardonnay. But this time it is beautifully presented, resting in its own little wooden box with some tasting notes underneath. And there's a beautiful aroma of wine all around. There's an oak floor and the walls are lined with exquisitely presented, delicious wine. How much is that bottle of Chardonnay there? And again, say a number out loud.

I've done this exercise with hundreds of people at seminars, and the average prices they come up with are about £6 in Sainsbury's, £4 in the corner shop and £8 in the wine merchant's. How do your three prices compare to those?

Now let me tell you about the actual bottle of wine I have here in front of me – exactly the same bottle of wine you've just given three prices for – and which other people have priced at £6, £4 and £8. But this time the wine is £141.

And yes, you did read that correctly, I did say £141. I paid £141 for it!

How a £141 bottle could change your life

Maybe the people that sold it to me for £141 know something about pricing that we ought to know too! They certainly know something that the workaholic selling it for £4 in the corner shop ought to know, don't they? And something Sainsbury's selling it at £6 ought to know. And even something the wine merchant selling it at £8 should know. If all those other people could sell it for £141 too, wouldn't their businesses be so much more successful?

Let me tell you about this £141 bottle. It wasn't sold in a shop. What happened was that one afternoon I was rung up by a friend and asked if I would like a free wine tasting at my house. The friend explained that she had just had a tasting, and that the wines were lovely. So I said yes. And within twenty minutes a very elegant middle aged woman arrived at my house in a fantastic sports car, and very carefully lifted out of the boot of her car two enormous aluminium boxes, rather like the kind photographers use to guard their equipment. One of the boxes was chilled and one of them wasn't. In the chilled box were eight bottles of white wine and in the other box were eight bottles of red wine.

She sat my wife and I down at our dining table and let us taste every wine in the box. She showed us how to savour them. She told us about each grape variety in great detail. She told us what other people's favourites were. She got us to put our favourite bottles to one side, and then complimented us on our good taste. And she made us feel very special. But never once did she tell us the price – and we didn't ask.

Sixteen small glasses of wine later we agreed that we wanted one bottle of our favourite white and one bottle of our favourite red. But it turned out that they don't sell individual bottles. In fact, they don't even sell mixed cases. Very smart that!

So we ended up buying a whole case – that's twelve bottles – of this Chardonnay.

And although they were *only* £11.69, let's call it £12, each – the case of twelve came to £141.00.

But that's not all. You see, we also ended up buying a case of our favourite red. So the cheque we wrote there and then was for almost £300. I should stress that we had never spent that sort of money on wine before – having previously been happy to buy a few bottles at a time from Oddbins or the supermarket. So this really was an astonishing outcome.

Now you tell me, which business you would rather run: a business selling this same bottle of wine for £4, or £8. Or a business able to charge £12 – and at the same time turn a customer who thought he only wanted two bottles into a £300 sale?

It's a tough question, I know, but it's a decision someone in your business has to make! What would you rather each of your sales was worth: £4, £6, £8, £12 or even £300? You decide.

The difference was a choice...

What was the difference between the business selling the wine at £4 and the business selling the same bottle at £12? Well, it certainly wasn't the wine itself – since that was exactly the same!

What was different was that the company selling it at £12:

- Chose to identify its ideal customers (professionals or wine lovers in this case).
- Chose to give those ideal customers what they really wanted (good wine made easy).
- Chose to transform the experience of buying into something much more enjoyable and memorable.
- Chose to develop a brilliant referral marketing system – remember, it all started because they asked my friend to telephone me.
- Chose to develop an equally brilliant sales system – including the script the elegant sales woman used and the things she did as we tasted.
- Chose to train their sales people brilliantly in how to use that system – and she was brilliant!
- Chose to have no shame, nervousness or hesitation about charging a premium price – £12 a bottle instead of £4.
- And they didn't just settle for charging higher per unit prices – but also created a pricing structure (i.e. only selling full, unmixed cases) that resulted in me paying them even more still!

And as a result of those choices they were able to make a lot more money … as the £300 cheque I gave them and the fantastic sports car the sales woman drove proved.

In the wine industry, if you choose to pile it high on the floor in a corner shop don't be surprised if you get £4. But if you choose to present it really professionally in somebody's home, don't be surprised if you get £12, or even £300.

... and it's your choice

Obviously the prices and the way things are done will be different at the two ends of the spectrum in your industry. But there will still be a spectrum. And there will still be the equivalent of the £4 end of the market and the £12 end of the market in your industry.

Where you are on that spectrum is entirely up to you. It's your choice.

If you're stuck with low prices and low profits, don't complain about it ... do something about it.

You choose what kind of business you run. You choose the kind of service you give to customers. You choose the things you do to set yourself apart from your competitors. You choose whether to be your industry's equivalent of a low margin corner store, or a higher margin wine merchant specialist, or a really high margin innovator who re-writes the rules about how to do things. And you choose how you price. In other words, you choose where you are on that spectrum.

And the better the choices you make in those areas, the higher your profits will be at your magic price.

You make those choices. The choices you made in the past have determined the profits you are making today. And the choices you make today will determine the profits you make in the future. Even more importantly, those choices will in turn have a big impact on the quality of your life. Get them right and you will live a richer, happier and less stressful life.

Key 13
Making your business less taxing 1

Earlier we saw that there are two main ways for a business to get its hands on more non-repayable cash. You can make more profitable sales, and get paid for them more quickly – which we have already looked at. You can also pay less tax and receive bigger tax refunds.

The challenge you should set your accountant is clear, you need help to reduce your tax bills to the absolute legal minimum, and increase your tax refunds to the absolute legal maximum.

And to do that you need to understand the differences between the four types of tax planning.

The four types of tax planning

ILLEGAL		LEGAL		
Tax evasion	No tax planning	Basic tax planning	Advanced tax planning
		Tax bills typically reduced by 5-25%	Tax bills typically reduced by 50-100%

Tax evasion
Keeping things 'off the books', working cash in hand, dodgy advice from some bloke down the pub and all other forms of deception and untruthfulness are, quite rightly, illegal. So I know

you would never contemplate them. Happily the remaining three types of tax planning are all entirely legal.

No tax planning

This is what many businesses do by default. They simply complete their tax returns and send them to the tax man having taken little or no prior action to arrange their affairs in such a way as to legally pay less tax. As a result they often end up paying the absolute maximum in tax, and never the absolute minimum.

Basic tax planning

This is what most businesses do, since it is what most of the accountants advising them are good at. And through basic tax planning strategies, such as incorporating the business, taking dividends rather than salaries and carefully timing when they spend money, they are often able to reduce their tax bills by between 5% and 25%.

Advanced tax planning

Historically this has been much less common. In fact, until recently it has only really been available to the very richest entrepreneurs. Indeed it is one of the things that has helped them to become very rich, since typically it can reduce tax bills by between 50% and 100%. However, that has all changed in the last few years, and now all good accountants can access the full range of advanced tax planning solutions on behalf of all their clients.

So the two questions you need to ask yourself are these:

1. Which of the three types of legal tax planning are you currently doing?
   (If your tax bills are not being reduced at all, then you are probably doing no tax planning. If they are being reduced

by less than 50% then you are probably only doing basic tax planning. And if they are being reduced by more than 50%, and perhaps even being eliminated completely, then you are probably already doing advanced tax planning.)

2. Are you 100% happy with the amount of tax you currently pay, or would you prefer to pay less?

If you would prefer to pay less, as understandably many people do, you need to talk to your accountant about your advanced tax planning options as a matter of urgency.

Think Harley Street

Just as most doctors are GPs, so most accountants are GPs (general practitioners) too. And in accountancy, as in medicine, your GP should always be your first port of call when you have a business or financial issue.

In most cases they will be able to help you. But sometimes they will need to bring in a specialist to ensure that you get the best possible results. In medicine they may refer you to a carefully chosen consultant from outside the practice, or even to Harley Street. While in the field of advanced tax planning they may refer you to an equally carefully chosen tax specialist from outside the practice.

Please regard this type of referral arrangement as a strength, rather than a weakness. After all, you wouldn't want your local GP performing open heart surgery on you, would you? You would want them to refer you to a specialist. And it is exactly the same with advanced tax planning.

This fact also explains why the last few months have seen an explosion in the advanced tax planning options available to ordinary businesses and taxpayers. And what has made that possible is the fact that most switched on accountants have started to forge strategic alliances with tax specialists. As a result they are now able to introduce clients to the sort of advanced tax planning that used to be the exclusive preserve of the mega rich.

The world of tax is changing almost daily at the moment. So if you haven't talked to your accountant about your advanced tax planning options in the last six months, do so today. It could help to put tens (if not hundreds) of thousands of pounds of extra non-repayable cash into your bank account.

Key 14
Making your business less taxing 2

As you have just seen, the world of tax is changing almost daily.

So it is impossible (and indeed unprofessional) for this or any other book to give you detailed tax advice.

Even so we can recommend in the strongest possible terms that you talk to your accountant to see to what extent the five tax planning ideas (some basic, some advanced) outlined below might be able to reduce your tax bills.

Idea 1 – Pay less tax when you get your money out tax efficiently

If you run a company then the basic ways to pay yourself are by salary, dividends and interest on loan accounts. In addition the business can also pay into your pension fund. But there are also a number of different types of Trust based profit extraction arrangements that can result in both you and the business paying much less in tax.

Perhaps even more importantly, these alternative arrangements usually also lead to far higher levels of motivation and productivity amongst the key people in your business. So they can have a profoundly positive effect on performance.

Idea 2 – Effectively pay no tax on expansion profits

Thanks to government incentives for growing businesses it is often possible to effectively earn between five and fifteen years of expansion profits free of tax. The exact savings and steps involved vary from case to case, but they usually involve some simple changes to the way your business is structured.

Expansion profits are essentially the profits you earn from major new products, major new services and other major new parts of your business.

So if you are planning on launching a major new product, service or arm to your business, this type of planning can make a very big difference. It won't change the tax you pay on your existing profits. But it can make your new profits effectively tax free.

Idea 3 – Get tax back on commercial property

By using the right multi-disciplinary team of accountant, lawyer and surveyor it is now often possible to identify big savings on the money you have already spent, or are about to spend, on commercial property.

These specialists will make a room by room physical inspection, and use their specialist knowledge to identify additional items that didn't appear in the original paperwork but which nevertheless it is still possible to claim tax relief for.

As a result you will probably receive a significant tax refund and/or your future tax bills will be significantly reduced.

Idea 4 – Receive up to £10,000 or more a year in tax credits

At the time of writing, if your household income is below about £58,000 then you may be entitled to child tax credits and/or working tax credits. And for a family with two children that can mean as much as an extra £9,700 a year in their bank account, while for families with more children the figure can be much higher (up to £14,300 a year if you have four children).

What's more, because of the particular way the system views income, you may be entitled to tax credits even if you think your income is too high. For example, HM Revenue & Customs estimate that nine out of ten families with children qualify for tax credits.

It is often also possible to take some simple steps to increase the level of tax credits available to you, so good advice really pays off.

But you need to act quickly … unlike ordinary tax returns, claims for tax credits are time sensitive, and by claiming early (i.e. before you think you might be able to get any tax credits) any future award can be maximised. Claiming late, on the other hand, will usually greatly reduce how much you eventually get.

Also, as a result of the June 2010 Budget, the tax credit system will become slightly less generous in 2011 and 2012, and will also involve more traps for the unwary. So acting quickly and taking good advice have never been more important.

Why bother? Well, the government recently estimated that £40 billion a year of legitimate tax credit entitlement is not actually being claimed. So it would be foolish to miss out on your share of that £40 billion, wouldn't it?

Idea 5 – Get a quadruple tax saving by incorporating

There are four types of tax savings you may be able to qualify for by converting your business into a limited company:

1. An initial windfall tax saving by 'capitalising goodwill'. This basically means selling your old business so that your new business owes you money. And you can then get that money out of your new business without paying a penny in income tax (although there is a special type of Capital Gains Tax charge, but that is usually a tiny fraction of the income tax saved).

2. Scope to receive as much as £10,000 a year in tax credits, even if your profits are much more than the tax credit upper threshold. For example, this can often be made possible by your new business repaying you some of the money it owes you for buying your old business, instead of paying you a salary. That way you still receive the same amount of net cash from the business. But as far as the system is concerned you are not receiving any 'income', so you qualify for full tax credits.

3. A recurring tax saving every year due to the differences between the ways incorporated and unincorporated businesses are taxed.

4. An additional tax saving by being able to use one of the Trust based profit extraction options described in Idea 1 above.

Don't accept 'no' for an answer. All five of the ideas above are legal. And at the time of writing they all work providing certain qualifying conditions are met. So if your accountant says they are not possible, please make sure that what they mean is either: (a) they no longer work because the tax rules have changed, or (b) they won't work for you because you don't meet the qualifying conditions.

Talk to another accountant if yours says, "That can't be done," when what they actually mean is, "I don't know how to do it." It is your money, and there is no way you should settle for paying a penny more in tax than you need to.

Part 2
Stress proofing the money stuff

Introduction

Imagine how much less stressful life would be if you knew that all the money issues in your family life were not only fully under control, but were also fully on track to pay for the life you really want to live.

More specifically, imagine how much less stressful life will be when you:

- Have a detailed plan for creating all the wealth you need to live your life to the full
- Are supported by a team of people who help you implement that plan
- Have a measuring system for making sure your plans are on track
- Can add an extra £1 million or more to your savings without even feeling it
- Know your retirement needs will be fully taken care of even if you don't have a pension
- Are able to shave thousands of pounds off your mortgage costs, and be completely mortgage free years ahead of time
- Will get every penny of the inheritance your parents worked so hard to build up in order to pass on to you
- And you also know that your children will be set up for life

This section will show you how to achieve all of this, and more.

Key 15
Get personal with your balance sheet

Which is more stressful: knowing that things are under control, or not knowing, and fearing the worst?

All business leaders understand the vital importance of having an up to date and accurate balance sheet to keep their businesses under control, but strangely, very few have extended the same logic to their personal affairs. And yet every business person we work with says that their family is more important to them than their business.

So the inescapable logic is that a personal balance sheet is even more important than a business balance sheet.

What is a personal balance sheet?

It is simply an up to date listing of everything you personally own (your assets) and everything you personally owe (your liabilities). There are columns containing those two sets of numbers for both you and your partner. For both columns there is a net total showing how much you are each worth. And there is also a total column showing your family's total assets, liabilities and net wealth.

Having an accurate personal balance sheet will do all of this for you:

Personal balance sheet

31 July 2010

	Mike Jones	Anne Jones	Combined
	£	£	£
ASSETS			
Main residence	600,000	600,000	1,200,000
Other property	798	1,550	2,348
Main business	57,500	192,500	250,000
Other business interests	6,501	5,500	12,001
Stocks and shares	64	32	96
Other investments	58	20	78
Current accounts	49	185	234
Deposit accounts	90	110	200
Other bank and building society accounts	252	513	765
Other assets	583	95	678
	665,895	800,505	1,466,400
LIABILITIES			
Mortgage	250,000	250,000	500,000
Loans	15	8	23
Other liabilities	13	11	24
	250,028	250,019	500,047
NET WORTH	£415,867	£550,486	£966,353

- It provides the starting point for you and your family's financial, wealth and retirement plans (which we will look at in more detail in the next section).
- It allows you to monitor your progress towards achieving those plans, replacing guesswork with fact.
- Where necessary it provides a wake up call about what needs to be done to make your plans achievable.

- It makes it easier to identify how much Inheritance Tax you might eventually be liable for, and how you can reduce or eliminate it.
- It also makes it easier for your family/executor/attorney to identify and deal with your estate should you either die or become incapacitated – greatly reducing the stress you cause your family at such an exceptionally difficult time.

The really big benefit

Having a personal balance sheet will also greatly reduce your stress levels because it brings clarity to your financial future and puts you firmly in control. If it shows a healthy position, you can relax in the knowledge that things are in hand. If it shows an unhealthy position, hallelujah! At least you will know about it before it is too late. Which means you can take corrective action. So once again you will be able to relax knowing that your corrective action plan will sort things out for you.

Either way, it is certainly far less stressful than not having a clue about your financial future, and losing sleep worrying about it.

And as a bonus...

Many people also say that producing a personal balance sheet for the first time, and seeing how much they are really worth, gives them a huge 'feelgood factor.'

Key 16
The five steps to wealth

OK, so now you know what you are really worth. Of course, if you're like most people, it's not enough. You want to be wealthier. And a sure-fire recipe for stress is not having a plan for making that happen. So you need a plan for increasing your personal wealth.

The five key steps to creating that plan are detailed below.

1. Assemble a Wealth Team of expert professionals – including your accountant and Independent Financial Adviser (IFA) – since your entire financial future is far too important a subject to be dealt with by ill-informed amateurs.

2. Work with your Wealth Team to review your personal balance sheet and related financial projections. As part of this you should consider such questions as:

   ■ How well are your assets performing – both in terms of generating income for you and increasing their capital value?
   ■ How can you improve that performance?
   ■ How can you improve the way your borrowings and other liabilities are structured?
   ■ Are you saving enough? In other words, is the gap between what you earn and what you spend sufficiently big? And if not, what can you do to earn more and/or spend less?

- How can you improve the way the risks to your personal wealth are managed?
- What can you do to reduce the risks to your wealth from Capital Gains Tax, Inheritance Tax and Stamp Duty?
- Will your current wealth grow sufficiently to pay for the future you dream of enjoying? And if it won't, what else do you need to do to ensure that it does?

3. Use the results of that review to develop a wealth management and improvement plan.

4. Implement your wealth management and improvement plan diligently – it is only by taking action that things will get better.

5. Repeat steps one to four regularly (typically once a year in most cases).

Is your IFA good enough?

You must have a really high quality Independent Financial Adviser on your Wealth Team.

If you already have an IFA, one quick test to see whether they are good enough is to consider these four simple questions:
1. Do you always feel that you understand 100% of the advice they give you?
2. Have they fully earned your trust, and do you always feel 100% confident about the advice they give you?
3. Do they always do what they say they are going to do, when they say they are going to do it?
4. Have they reviewed your affairs in detail in the last twelve months?

If the answer to any of these questions is no, I suggest you ask your accountant to recommend another IFA.

Brutal it may be. But you owe it to your family not to settle for second best, don't you?

Key 17
Your wealth starter for ten

This book is not the place for a detailed account of what should be on your wealth management and improvement plan – partly because that is too much for any one book, partly because, as a business owner, you already know much of what needs doing, and partly because that is the job of your Wealth Team.

Therefore, we will restrict ourselves here to looking at some of the aspects of the plan that many people who don't yet have a great Wealth Team in place most often overlook or get wrong. So here are a few key points to get the ball rolling for you.

Retirement matters

If you are lucky you will get old! And if you are very lucky you will have twenty, thirty, perhaps even forty or more years of retirement. If your retirement is going to be a happy one, money matters (of course your health and relationships probably matter more, but money does definitely matter). So financial planning for your retirement is not an optional extra, it is essential.

But you may not need a conventional pension

In fact, planning for your retirement doesn't necessarily involve a conventional pension (which is good news if you are sceptical about them). Instead, it is about accumulating wealth that earns you passive income in your retirement, or that you can cash-in and live off the sale proceeds. You may decide to accumulate your wealth in stocks and shares, bonds, or other financial investments. Or you may prefer something a little more tangible, such as property. Either way, your Wealth Team will help you make the right choices, and your personal balance sheet will help you keep the score.

Your business as a key retirement asset

As an entrepreneur, you have one asset that most people will never have – your own business. So the two keys for you are to maximise the value of that business, and to maximise its saleability. The way to maximise value is obvious: you need to make your business more successful and profitable. But maximising its saleability can be even more of a challenge.

One of the problems is that even a very profitable business will be hard to sell for its full value if you are the only person that knows how to run it. Part of the solution is to start running the business with its eventual sale in mind: for example, by ensuring that any skeletons in the cupboard are dealt with and that the business is systemised so that it can run equally well in your absence.

The other part of the solution is to talk to a corporate finance professional who specialises in selling businesses like yours. Most of them only charge when you appoint them to actually sell your business. So there will probably be no charge for picking their brains in the first instance. And it will give you a much clearer idea of the issues you will need to consider. Ask your accountant to recommend one.

How much is your business worth?

If you don't know, you need to find out. After all, its eventual sale could hold the key to your entire financial future. So you need to get a handle on its value today, and put that in your personal balance sheet. And you need to repeat that process regularly to see whether its value is progressing as you would like it to.

Go tax free

Now that income tax and Capital Gains Tax rates look set to be at record high levels, it is more important than ever to make the very most of tax free investment vehicles such as ISAs. For example, if you invest £10,000 a year into an ISA for twenty years, and it grows by 10% a year, you will have an investment worth £572,750. Better still, you will pay no income tax or capital gains tax on any of the income or capital gains you earn from that investment. And now that the annual limits on how much you can invest in an ISA have been substantially increased, for many people ISAs are now becoming an even more important part of their retirement planning.

And get even more help from the tax man

Talk to your accountant about what else you can do to reduce or eliminate your own and your family's tax bills. Some of the commonly overlooked options at the time of writing include:

- Shifting income between family members to ensure that as much income as possible is taxed at the lowest rates of income tax.

■ Claiming tax credits.

■ Making the most of specialist investment opportunities that earn you a sizeable profit if the investment goes well, and give you a tax refund that is larger than the amount you invested if the investment performs badly.

■ Structuring the way you buy your next house so that little or no Stamp Duty and Land Tax is payable. (Remember, on a £500,000 house Stamp Duty will normally be £20,000, and on a £1 million house it will normally be £40,000. So the savings can be very substantial.)

■ And the many other ideas suggested in Key 14.

Key 18
Dramatically reduce your mortgage and its cost

If you want to strengthen your personal financial position, one of the first places you should focus your attention is your mortgage. For most people, their mortgage is one of the biggest expenses they will incur in their entire life.

For example, you will pay £93,000 in interest for every £100,000 you borrow at an interest rate of 6% on a 25 year repayment mortgage. And that is in addition to the £100,000 capital that you also need to repay. So taking out a mortgage of, say, £300,000 will actually cost you an extra £279,000 in lifetime interest charges.

Most people realise that they can dramatically reduce this lifetime interest cost by making occasional and regular overpayments. And that is precisely why, as interest rates have fallen recently, many people have chosen to maintain their monthly payments at their historical levels in order to start making overpayments each month.

But some business owners have another really easy way to pay off their mortgages much more quickly and for a much smaller interest cost.

Just for sole traders

If you are a sole trader many mortgage providers will now give you a business offset mortgage that allows you to offset the money in your business bank account against your residential mortgage.

The main benefit of having this kind of mortgage is that your business current account effectively earns tax free interest at the mortgage interest rate. And this in turn means that:

■ The total lifetime interest cost of your mortgage will be reduced

■ And your mortgage will be paid off early

Even on quite small mortgages and business bank account balances these benefits can be very significant.

For example, offsetting an average of £30,000 in a business bank account against a 25 year, £100,000 mortgage with a 6% interest rate will reduce the overall lifetime mortgage interest cost by £40,000 and pay off the mortgage eight years early.

So, if saving that sort of money and being debt free earlier appeals, take a close look at how a business offset mortgage might work for you.

Key 19
Six ways to spend less without even noticing it

Mortgage interest costs may well be your biggest single item of personal lifetime expenditure. But there are plenty of other large expenses too. Designer clothes and shoes, electrical items, computer games, gadgets, jewellery, cars and holidays: the list is almost endless.

So here are six practical ways to spend less in these sorts of areas without it having any negative effect on your perception of your own standard of living.

Keep a twenty-eight day list

Want to buy something that is not absolutely essential? Write it down, and wait twenty-eight days before you actually buy it. If you still really want it on day twenty-eight, go ahead. But the chances are that most of the things on your list will no longer seem like such a good idea so you'll decide not to buy them, and save yourself a fortune.

Go online

The internet is a great place to find low prices. And, of course, once you have found them, you can either buy online, or simply use the online price to negotiate a concession from a traditional bricks and mortar retailer. (Last Friday I did exactly this and my local travel agent gave me £160 off the price of a holiday for two in order to match an internet price. All I said to them was, "I've seen it for £160 less on the internet. If you can match that price I will give you the order today." And they did, without any unpleasantness!)

Negotiate a lower price

You do it in your business life, so do it in your personal life too. It won't generally work in a newsagent or other places where you are standing in a queue to spend a few pennies or pounds! But where the amounts are larger you will be surprised at how often you can negotiate a better deal. And, in fact, don't just settle for a lower price. Ask "what is your best price?"

Get extra stuff thrown in

Once you have negotiated the best price, don't stop there. Also ask them to throw in some other related items. For example, if you are buying golf clubs, ask them to throw in some balls. Related items are often of high value to you, but low cost to them so getting them free will save you a lot of money while costing the seller very little – making them excellent concessions for everybody.

Cut up or freeze your credit cards

If overspending on credit cards is your downfall, cut them up. And if that is too extreme, put them in a plastic container full of water and freeze them. That way they will always be on hand if you really need them. But since they will need to thaw out before you can use them, you won't fall foul of any reckless impulse spending.

Forget about keeping up with the Joneses

As Lily Tomlin said, "The trouble with the rat race is that, even if you win, you're still a rat." So why spend more and more of your hard-earned money on ostentatious displays of wealth that are more about trying to look richer than others than they are about actually making you happy? The reality is that there will always be people who are better off than you, trying to look richer than them is a game you are always going to lose.

Instead of playing that game, how about deciding to live your life for you? Choose to move the focus of your life from 'excess' to 'enough'. Enough to meet your needs, enough to make you happy, and rearrange your spending accordingly.

Key 20
The easiest way to get an extra £1 million

In the previous section we looked at your larger types of expenditure. Now let's look at the small stuff that can have an even more profound impact.

If you really needed to, I bet you could save £5 a day from your daily expenditure, couldn't you?

It might be a case of not buying that latte and sandwich on the way to work, and replacing them with a flask and packed lunch from home. It might be the vending machine drinks and snacks, lunchtime beer and daily newspaper that go. Or the branded food that you replace with own label equivalents. It may even be something else.

But before you object with 'but those are my little luxuries', let's just work out what they are really costing you. That £5 a day is actually £1,300 a year, which means:

■ Even without any interest or compound growth, it adds up to £52,000 over a 40 year working life.

■ If you were able to invest that £1,300 a year at 10%, by the end of a 40 year working life it would have grown to a staggering £575,370.

It's your money

The real cost to you and your family of that latte and sandwich could actually be somewhere between £50,000 and half a million pounds. And if your partner can also save £5 a day from their spending, then the combined amounts at stake for the two of you will be somewhere between £100,000 and £1 million!

Do you like your £5 a day luxuries enough to sacrifice that sort of money for them? Or would it make your life better if you were able to spend up to a million pounds on other even more important things?

If the answer to that second question is yes, what adjustments are you going to make to save £5 a day?

Key 21
Make illness easier for your loved ones

Imagine how unhappy and stressed your loved ones will be if you become really ill. It's almost unimaginable, isn't it? Sadly there's nothing I can tell you that will lessen the pain, but there is one thing I can urge you to do that will greatly reduce the stress.

Power of Attorney

Have you made things easier for your family by putting a Power of Attorney in place?

Essentially a Power of Attorney is a formal document that nominates a trusted individual to deal with your financial affairs and property in the unfortunate event of you being incapacitated, either physically or mentally.

And because this makes things so much easier for your family, they are widely regarded as a very important part of good financial management.

Up to October 2007 it was possible to set up an Enduring Power of Attorney, and if you had done so by that date then it should remain effective. But if you hadn't already set one up by October 2007, you will need to set up a new style Lasting Power of Attorney.

Setting up a Power of Attorney won't make anyone rich (apart, perhaps, from your lawyer). But it will reduce the stress and hassle for your family should anything unpleasant happen to you.

Get mum and dad in on the act too

It's not just you that should have a Power of Attorney; your parents, and any other loved ones who might possibly become ill, should have them too.

That way *your* stress levels will be greatly reduced should anything happen to *them*.

Key 22
Making old age and death easier for your loved ones

Illness is not inevitable. But getting older and eventually dying certainly are, and they can also be extremely stressful, especially for the people left behind to pick up the pieces. But there are things you can do to reduce the financial related stresses.

Prevent care fees from stealing your legacy

Should you, or any of your family members, ever have to go into a care home, you may find that the vast majority of your savings (that you are probably planning to leave to your family) is taken from you by the government in the form of care home fees.

At the time of writing the facts are these:

- If you have assets or capital in excess of around £23,000 you have to pay 100% of the cost of care home fees.
- Typical care fees are £30,000 a year or more, so the cost can mount up frighteningly quickly.
- As a result, one in five people in the UK have to sell their assets, including the family home, to fund care home fees.

The same rules also apply to your parents and other family members. So their estates – and therefore your inheritance – can be seriously eroded by these charges.

Ten years in care, for example, can easily add up to a £300,000 loss to the estate. And if your parents only started off with an estate of, say, £325,000, then there would only be £25,000 left to pass on to you as the next generation. So, in effect, you will have suffered what amounts to a 92% tax bill on your inheritance.

Just thinking about that is enough to make my blood pressure and stress levels rise dramatically. And I suspect you feel the same.

But that is not the end of the bad news...

Prevent the taxman stealing your legacy

The 92% of your inheritance you would lose in the previous example is before any formal Inheritance Tax starts to take its slice of the action.

Remember, Inheritance Tax has long been regarded by many as a very unfair form of taxation. After all:

- It effectively charges you up to an extra 40% in double tax on money that you have already paid tax on.
- You will suffer Inheritance Tax of up to 40% when you receive an inheritance in your lifetime.
- And you will suffer it again when you leave an inheritance on your death.

For example, even if your parents never go into care, if they have worked and saved hard to leave you a legacy, that legacy could be decimated by Inheritance Tax. So you may end up receiving only a fraction of what they had hoped you would receive. Then, when your children eventually inherit from you the same money will be taxed again and they will receive even less.

The good news

The good news, however, is that care fees and Inheritance Tax are in reality entirely voluntary. With the right advice there is much you can do to greatly reduce or eliminate them, so don't allow yourself and your family to suffer unnecessarily.

Get urgent advice on how much extra money it is possible to put in your bank account through suitable care fee and Inheritance Tax planning for your parents and other older loved ones. Also find out how much extra money it is possible to give to your children and other younger loved ones by suitable care fee and Inheritance Tax planning for your own life.

A word of warning

There is a right and a wrong way to protect yourself from care fees and Inheritance Tax.

The wrong way is to syphon money off from the older person's bank account, transfer the house from their name while they still live in it, and any number of other naïve and often dodgy tactics suggested by the bloke down the pub.

The right way is to get proper advice on the legitimate ways to use trusts, etc., to protect your family's assets from the ravages of care fees and Inheritance Tax.

Tomorrow may be too late

Usually care fee and Inheritance Tax planning arrangements need to be put in place well before the need for care, or death, is imminent. So the ideal time to take action is today. Tomorrow may well be too late.

Key 23
Get the very best from your accountant

Have you ever done something, and then found out afterwards that you could have got a much better deal, price or result if you had done it differently? It's always a risk, isn't it? When what's at stake is small, this kind of risk is annoying, but you can probably live with it. But when there's a lot at stake, really large amounts of money for instance, the risk of messing things up can be really stressful.

When it comes to the financial side of business and life, the key to eliminating those kinds of risks and stresses is, of course, to make sure you talk to your accountant before you rush into anything. By talking to them in good time they may be able to help you to:

- Save time or money;
- Get a better solution;
- Avoid the risks and pitfalls;
- Enjoy the most favourable tax treatment;
- Or in some other way get a better result.

On the other hand, if you only talk to them after the event it will probably be too late.

So as soon as any of the things on the lists below become relevant to you, or you even start to consider them, you should talk to your accountant immediately: and certainly well before you take any decisions or actions. In each case the list also suggests where to start your discussions with them.

Unhappy with the performance of your business?

1. Unhappy with your sales and/or profits? Talk to your accountant about how to make the most of the eight profit drivers, your magic price and the many other ideas in Part 1.

2. Unhappy with your cashflow? Remember the importance of non-repayable sources of money, and talk to them about direct debits and the other issues raised in Key 8.

3. Unhappy with your business and/or personal tax bills? Remember to ask them about the sort of advanced tax planning options covered in Keys 13, 14 and 17.

4. Don't feel you have your finger on the pulse? Get your accountant's help in finding the 20% of customers, products and markets that generate 80% of your results (Key 2), benchmarking your business against your industry (Key 5), setting targets and analysing your variances against them, identifying your Key Success Drivers, producing a One Page Plan (Key 6) to bring them all together, and mapping the trends. And then use all those insights to create an improvement action plan.

5. Want to make better decisions and get better results? Ask your accountant to meet with you on a regular basis to discuss your One Page Plan, bring a fresh pair of eyes to your decision making process, and make you accountable for your action plan so that everything gets done and things get better.

Borrowing, banking and finance

1. Remortgaging? Consider the huge savings from an offset mortgage as discussed in Key 18.

2. Thinking of changing bank? Ask your accountant who they recommend.

3. Thinking of borrowing? Discuss the available options, and which is right for you.

4. Thinking of leasing or some other form of asset finance? Again, discuss your best options.

5. Other forms of refinancing? Again, discuss your best options.

Business expansion

1. Launching a major new product, service or division? Talk to your accountant about the possibility of paying no tax on your expansion profits as discussed in Key 14.

2. Setting up a new business? Evaluate the alternative structures.

3. Buying a business? Ask them to 'due diligence' it so there are no nasty surprises. This will also help you to negotiate the best possible terms.

4. Setting up a limited company? Make sure all the i's are dotted and t's crossed.

5. Turning your business into a Limited Company? Talk to them about the four types of tax savings mentioned in Key 14.

You and your employees

1. Paying key people over and above their standard salary? Ask your accountant about the alternatives to salary, bonus and dividends discussed in Key 14.

2. Making additional payments to the owners? Again, discuss all the options.

3. Appointing a new Director, or parting company with an existing Director? Make sure all the formalities are dealt with.

4. Employing a family member? Structure their pay properly.

5. Taking on a sub-contractor? Make sure you don't fall foul of the very complicated rules.

6. Setting up a profit sharing scheme? Do it tax efficiently.

7. The business is buying assets for the personal use of the owners/employees? Real care is needed.

Cars

1. Buying or leasing a car? Ask your accountant about the tax, accounting and cashflow implications, and also about getting the best deal.

2. Using a car for business? Maximise your claims.

Business ownership and structure

1. Major changes to what the business does?

2. Changing shareholders/partners?

3. Changing business structure?

4. Changing shareholder/partnership agreements?

5. Transferring or selling shares?

6. Issuing new shares?

There are some crucial legal, commercial and tax issues in all these areas, so good advice is essential.

Getting out

1. Selling all or part of your business? Ask your accountant to recommend a really good corporate finance specialist.

2. Thinking about retiring? Evaluate the state of your finances and what needs to be done to ensure you can afford to retire in the style you wish.

3. Setting up or changing pension arrangements? Consider the alternatives to pensions as discussed in Key 17.

General tax and accounts

1. Changing accounting system?

2. Exceeding the VAT threshold for the first time?

3. Being notified of a VAT or PAYE visit?

4. Changing your VAT arrangements?

All of these contain enormous pitfalls for the unwary, so talk to the experts immediately.

Other business issues

1. Appointing consultants or other professional advisers? Ask your accountant to recommend who is best for you.

2. Exporting or importing? Make sure the customs, currency, cashflow, risk and reporting issues are dealt with properly.

3. Winning a major new contract or customer? Do the right credit checks and set the right credit limits.

Property and investments

1. Buying, selling, refurbishing, extending or improving commercial property? Ask your accountant about how to get the most favourable tax treatment. For example, it may involve a multi-disciplinary team of accountant, lawyer and surveyor reclassifying what you buy. It may involve

structuring the transaction so that no stamp duty and land tax is payable. Or it may involve reducing your Capital Gains Tax bills.

2. Buying or selling a home? Ditto.

3. Buying or selling other assets? Ditto.

4. Other major investment? Ask your accountant what specialist advisers you need to talk to.

Family

1. Family income reduced? Ask your accountant about claiming tax credits.

2. Want to be richer? Work with them to implement the ideas in Keys 15 and 16.

3. Want to spend less and save more? Follow the advice in Keys 19 and 20.

4. Writing a will? Make sure it minimises your Inheritance Tax bills.

5. Suspect that you may receive an inheritance at some time in the future? Check that the Inheritance Tax and care fee planning issues have been dealt with by the people who want to leave you the inheritance (Key 22).

6. Making large gifts to family and friends? Get the tax and care fee angles covered.

7. Receiving a large windfall such as a lottery win? Get the right tax, investment and protection advice (Key 16).

8. Getting married or divorced, moving abroad or other major changes in your personal circumstances? Check out the implications, issues and opportunities for your tax and broader financial affairs.

You will probably get better results

It may not always be possible to get you better results in all of these areas. But very often it will be. And even if your accountants can't personally help, they will probably be able to introduce you to an expert who can.

Part 3
Stress proofing the personal stuff

Introduction

OK, so now you've addressed most of the business and money related causes of stress. But let's face it, there's still going to be some stress in your life. It's inevitable (and actually quite a good thing, by the way). Families, neighbours, food, politics, health, relationships, traffic and all the other things that make up life can all cause stress.

So in Part 3 you will discover:

■ How to reduce and prevent the other types of stress, and

■ How to deal with, and even benefit from, the stresses in your life no matter how they are caused.

Key 24
Achieve life–work balance in ten minutes

I refuse to call it work–life. It should be life–work. And that's what achieving it entails – a life–work, unless of course, you've read this idea.

One of the most pernicious things about stress is the way we don't notice how it switches our attention away from what we value and love in life until it's too late. So here are some clues to look out for as indicators that work stress is stomping all over your life–work balance:

1. Do you feel like your day is spent dealing with difficult people and difficult tasks?
2. Do you feel that those you love don't have a clue what's going on with you and you don't have a clue what's going on with them?
3. Do you regularly make time for activities that nourish your soul?
4. Do you feel you could walk out the door of your house and no one would notice you were gone until the mortgage had to be paid?

Yes, you guessed it? Number 3 was the trick question. Answer yes to that one and you're probably all right. Answer yes to the rest and you could be in trouble.

In a nutshell: make sure you're putting time and effort into the people and activities that make your heart sing and it really is very difficult to buckle under the effect of stress.

But I think too much emphasis is put on the stress caused by the work part of the equation and not enough placed on the stress caused by the life bit. Everyone assumes that all we need is less work, more life and all would be harmonious balance. I'm not so sure.

Where it has gone wrong for so many, women especially, is that they've cleared enough time for the life part of the equation but not taken into account that it isn't necessarily restful or enjoyable. This is no idle observation. Research shows that men's stress hormones tend to fall when they get home whereas women's stay high after the working day, presumably because they get home to confront a dozen chores and hungry kids. Your children may be the reason you get out of bed in the morning but you need to accept that spending time with them is not necessarily any less stressful than work – in fact, it often makes work seem like a walk in the park. More time with your kids is not necessarily the answer.

More time with yourself, very probably, is.

That old saying is true – if you don't look after yourself, you can't look after anyone else. And all it takes is just ten minutes a day. Ten minutes of selfishness every day is enough to make a profound difference in your ability to achieve a life-balance that works.

Why not get started by trying this: designate Saturday 'family day' and Sunday afternoon 'selfish' time. We can usually find an hour or so on Sunday afternoon to spend on ourselves – just don't let it get filled with chores or others' agendas.

Key 25
The positive side of stress

So you're stressed? Be grateful. Stress makes life a lot sweeter when you learn to manage it right. Better sex, sharper mind, longer life – stress does all this – which is why so many of us are addicted to it.

Nearly half of all people report to being more stressed today than they were five years ago; over three-quarters of people consider stress to be intrinsic to their jobs. But let's look at the positives. Some stress is good, even necessary.

Stress keeps you young

When you're stressed your adrenal glands produce a hormone called dehydroepiandrosterone – known as DHEA to its friends – which has been shown to keep mice alive longer. It was also noted that the same mice had more luxuriant coats. The hormone is thought to build collagen and elastin (the building blocks of the skin) and this stimulates a younger looking appearance. (The beauty industry has latched onto this and is trying to develop products that contain DHEA. You're ahead of the game, you produce your own.)

Stress makes you smart

DHEA makes your mind sharper. Chronic stress makes you forgetful but short-term stress can make your brain work better for short periods.

Stress lifts your mood

If you're feeling down in the dumps, a bit of stress isn't necessarily terrible. It could be just what you need to perk you up again. Stress forces you to make decisions and take responsibility. Experts believe this protects us from falling into a state of depression. A recent study found that short doses of the stress hormone cortisol protect some people against depression in the way that anti-depressants regulate mood. Too much cortisol leads to extreme exhaustion, but just a little bit is fine.

Stress improves your sex life

Let's hear it for our old friend, DHEA. Women with a low libido who were given doses of DHEA got more interested again. It turns out that low levels of stress are linked to control of sex drive. Moderate stress releases DHEA and this affects libido positively.

Stress keeps you alive

A study carried out at the University of Texas showed that people with few pressures are up to 50% more likely to die within ten years of quitting work than those who faced major responsibility. People under regular pressure tend to take better control of their lives and as a result suffer fewer conditions linked to failing finances, poor relationships and employment problems.

Life is innately stressful. Even if you lock yourself in your bedroom for the foreseeable future, stress will find you. Stress is caused by change and life changes even if you withdraw from it and hide under the bed. But by learning to manage stress, and use it to your advantage, you can find it motivates, energises and spurs you on to a richer and more fulfilling life. Remember there's only one thing worse for you than too much stress, and that's too little.

Why not get started by trying this…
Relaxation is easier in the dark. Any time you need to de-stress instantly, put your palms over your closed eyes and imagine you are enveloped in black velvet.

Key 26
Avoid the perfection trap

Your need to be 'perfect' isn't about perfection, it's about staying in control. And staying in control is not a virtue if it's making you miserable.

I have a friend who recently ran her first marathon. And she did run the whole way, never once slowing down to a walk. She felt fabulous for about six hours afterwards – she deserved to. Then the self-doubt began – she should have run faster, pushed herself more, achieved a better time. She couldn't stop beating herself up for not doing it 'better'.

I was dumbstruck. She looks better than me, earns more than me, achieves more than me, but a small voice inside constantly tells her that she's just not good enough. Does it have to be that way? I think perfectionists can achieve just as much if they let that voice go for good.

Only you can learn to ignore the little voice. If you don't, you'll never be able to relax properly. Often that little voice belongs to someone we know, often someone who brought us up, who has no idea of the complexity of our world. Give it up!

■ Ration your perfectionist behaviour. You probably won't ever lose it completely. However, you can limit it. One woman I know whose energy levels had plummeted finally made the connection between her habit of staying up late reading and answering emails and her inability to get to sleep (duh!). So now she allows herself two nights a week to check emails late. Go through your own life working out where you can cut down or cut out perfectionist habits.

- Lose your fear of the person who made you this way. Even if you were always the sort of kid who liked to colour code your books, no one becomes a perfectionist unaided. Someone somewhere had high expectations of you. Accept something pretty basic: if you haven't earned their unconditional approval by now, you probably never will. Let it go. And if you can't, get therapy.

- Walk barefoot in the park. Remember Jane Fonda begging Robert Redford to stop being such a stuffed shirt and to walk barefoot in Central Park? You could try the same – just to see if you like it. You probably won't – but it might teach you something valuable: that nobody cares but you. Whatever your version of mad devil-may-care spontaneity – asking friends to dinner and ordering a takeaway curry, or letting your roots show, or putting on a few kilos, or refusing to take the kids swimming on Sunday morning because you simply can't be bothered – go on, do it. The kids will not implode with disappointment. The world will not fall apart. Slip up and nothing happens.

No one cares if you're perfect but you (and the person who made you this way, see above, but we've dealt with them already).

Key 27
Find an hour a day to play

No seriously, is that too much to ask?

Shut your eyes. Breathe deeply. Picture what you'd do today if you had a whole hour each day to yourself to spend doing exactly what you wanted.

Here's a question worth asking

You can put the 'desirable' things we'd like to spend an hour doing into two categories:

1. The stuff we yearn to do because it's relaxing and fun.

2. The stuff that's usually prefixed with a sense of 'ought to' because we know the rewards are worth it.

In the first category is lying in bed watching a movie, in the second is going for a run or quality time with the kids. We need to find the time for both. But both categories tend to get shunted to the sidelines of our lives because of general business.

Nothing in your life will change unless you take action. If you don't take the time to exercise, if you consistently allow family and work demands to be more important than your continual good health, then at best you'll be more vulnerable to illness; at worst you'll be fat (and still more vulnerable to illness).

This goes for life dreams that fall into the first category, like writing a novel or learning Russian. These have been called 'depth activities' because they add meaning to our lives. Here's the big question: how will you feel in five years' time if you haven't at least tried to achieve one of your dreams?

First get the big picture...

Get out your diary and write down everything you're expected to make happen in the next month. This could take some time. Include everything from work projects, organising baby-sitters, buying birthday presents, decorating the bathroom, taxing the car, medical appointments.

OK, finished? Right, go through the list and mark the items that you can delegate to someone else. Be honest. Items you *can* delegate, not the ones that no one else wants to do, or the ones that no one else will do as well as you. Don't worry. You don't have to hand over all these tasks, just 10% of them.

Now you've offloaded 10% of your work for the next month, think about dumping 10% of what you have to do every day. Jot down your 'tasks' for tomorrow. Quickly, without thinking too much, run through them marking each entry.

A Must do
B Should do
C Could do

Now knock two of the Bs off the list and three of the Cs off and replace them with an activity that you know would de-stress you or add depth to your life. Mark it with a whacking great 'A'. Soon, giddy with success, you'll be prioritising yourself all of the time. Well, at least for an hour a day. Life really is too short to wallow in the C-list – feeling busy but achieving nothing that matters.

Key 28
Dealing with the week from hell

Facing the week from hell? Here's how to survive it.

Don't catastrophise

On really busy days with multiple deadlines, I've got to the stage where I'm scared to answer the phone in case it's someone demanding something else of me. Then I made a conscious decision to stop being a victim. Every time a negative thought crosses your brain, cancel it out with a positive one. This takes practice. An easy way to do it is to develop a mantra to suit whatever crisis you're in today and that you say to yourself repeatedly every time your mind goes into tailspin. Right now, I have to pick the kids up from school in half an hour. I have four weeks to my deadline for this book and I have done approximately half the number of words I promised myself I'd write today. My mantra is, 'I am serenely gliding towards my deadline and everything will get done.' Every time panic hits, I chant this to myself and feel much better.

Master the only question that matters

The 'best use' question was taught to me by my first boss and it is invaluable in negotiating your way through any day with dozens of calls on your time. It helps you to prioritise 'on the run', sometimes quite ruthlessly. On the morning of manic days decide what you've got to achieve that day and if anything interrupts, ask yourself 'Is this the best use of my time, right now?' If the answer is no, take a rain-check and come back to it later. So if a friend calls you at work, nine times out of ten, you won't chat then, you'll call her back at a more convenient time – unless, of course, she is very upset about something, in which case talking to her *is* the best use of your time.

Always under promise

A lot of stress is of our own making. Life coach Thomas Leonard says, 'One of the biggest mistakes is to tell people what they want to hear, give them what they think they want, without thinking if it's feasible for you. You over promise results you can't deliver without a lot of stress. And of course, if you don't deliver, not only are you stressed, *they* are, too.' Leonard's advice is to under promise rather than over promise. That way your friends are delighted when you turn up at the party you said you couldn't make and your boss thinks you're wonderful when you get the report finished a day early rather than a week late. Make it your rule from now on to be absolutely realistic about how long it's going to take you to get things done. And until you get expert at this, work out the time you reckon it will take you to complete any task and multiply it by 1.5.

Why not get started by trying this...
Keep a time log of your working week so you finally get a realistic idea of how long it takes you to complete all your usual activities. This means you stop kidding yourself about how quickly you will perform tasks in an imperfect world – where you're interrupted frequently –and you'll reduce your stress levels hugely.

Key 29
Relaxation – what we can learn from the cavemen

There's nothing wrong with stress. We're designed to get stressed. It's how we deal with it that's the problem. Coping with stress should be simple. My central message to you can be summarised in one sentence. Get stressed – relax.

So why are we facing an epidemic of stress? The answer lies in the way we interpret the word 'relax'. Remember that stress developed in order for us to deal with danger. When faced with something that scares us (more likely nowadays to be a to-do list running into double figures rather than the sabre-toothed tigers that ate our ancestors), we release adrenaline, this in turn causes the release of noradrenaline and cortisol and these three hormones together sharpen our wits, release energy to our muscles and divert resources from one part of the body to the bits where you need it most. Which is why you feel twitchy when you're very stressed and can't sit still. The adrenaline coursing through your body would have been just dandy in helping you cope with the sabre-toothed tiger but is a bit of an overreaction when your boss has caught you booking your holiday on the internet rather than working on the sales report. All those hormones get the job done. But rest is essential to repair and recover from their effect.

So what do we do now after a stressful day? We are likeliest to celebrate with alcohol, a cigarette, coffee (all of which trigger another stress response). Or even worse, after a stressful situation, we throw ourselves straight into another one. This means that our bodies are bathed in stress hormones for far longer than was ever intended.

The body's hormones work in delicate balance. When the three main stress hormones are fired they affect the levels of all the others, notably insulin (which regulates sugar levels and energy) and serotonin (the happy hormone which affects mood and sleep). When they go awry over long periods of time, the results can be disastrous for our health, both mental and physical.

Five minutes every hour

See your day not as a long purgatory of stress but as lots of small stress responses punctuated with mini-relaxation breaks. As a rough rule, every waking hour should have five minutes of pleasure. So after every hour of working, take a few minutes to do something pleasurable – answer an email, stretch your shoulders, have a cup of tea. Can't leave your desk? Spend a few minutes dreaming of something that makes you happy.

Fifteen minutes every day

Practise active relaxation – listening to music, yoga, sex, dancing. TV is passive and doesn't count.

Three hours every week

At least three hours every week should be spent doing an activity you love. It should be calming, and non-work orientated. I make it a rule that it only counts as my three hours if I can do it without make-up. In other words, it doesn't count if it involves people that I feel I have to make an effort with.

> *Why not get started by trying this...*
> *Next time you're waiting in a queue, or for traffic lights to change or for your lift to arrive, see it as an opportunity for a mini-break. Take some deep breaths, feel the tension flow out of your body and your shoulders drop. People who make an effort to do this report being less stressed in a week.*

Key 30
Make 'just say no' your new mantra

A huge amount of stress is caused by the inability to say no. The result? We end up running to other people's agendas.

Now and then, all of us have to do things that don't benefit us much in order to feel that we're pulling our weight. But if it's a daily occurrence then we're going to get run down and ill. Worse, we're going to get seriously fed up.

Try this quiz. Answer True or False for each of these questions:

1. I can't relax until I finish all the things I have to do.
2. If I wasn't doing favours for other people most days, I wouldn't think much of myself.
3. I seldom say no to a work colleague or family member who asks a favour of me.
4. I often find myself changing my own plans or working day to fit in with other people's wants.
5. I rarely, if ever, feel comfortable with what I've accomplished.
6. I often feel I'm so exhausted that I don't have time for my own interests.
7. I feel guilty relaxing.

8. I find myself saying 'yes' to others and inside a voice is saying 'no, no, no'.

9. I honestly believe that if I stop doing things for others they'd think less of me.

10. I find it hard to ask other people to do things for me.

Add up the number of Ts you scored. If your score is between seven and ten, you think it more important to please others than to please yourself. If it's between four and six, you should be careful. You're on the slippery slope to terminal niceness. If your score is three or less, you're good at saying no and keep your own needs in balance with others. You should aim for a score of under three.

Here are some ways to get your score under three:

- List your top ten no's, the things you want to eliminate from your life. Start each sentence 'I will no longer…'

- Think of situations where you need to say no to improve your life. Imagine yourself in these situations saying no. Practise the exercise in front of a mirror if necessary. (This is brilliant. The experience of actually saying no out loud, albeit in private, makes it much easier in real-life situations.)

- Whenever you're asked to do anything, ask yourself: 'Do I really want to do this?' rather than 'Should I do this?' If the answer is no, then let someone else pick up the baton.

Why not get started by trying this…
If you just can't say no, try an intermediate stage. Next time someone asks you to do something, say: 'I'm not sure, let me get back to you.' The breather is often enough to stiffen your resolve.

Key 31
Are you too stressed to be happy?

Stress saps energy and eventually our enjoyment of life. Stress makes us unhappy without us even realising it. Do you accept the stressed-out state as just the way you are? Does it have to be this way?

The World Health Organization's definition of good health is not just an absence of disease but the 'presence of *emotional* and physical well-being' (my italics). So are you healthy? Few of us can remember when we last felt 100% emotionally and physically well. And the chances are that it's stress that's bringing you down.

Here are some questions to help you pinpoint how stress is affecting your well-being, perhaps without you realising it.

Imagine what it would be like to live without irritation and self-blame. Recognising these emotions as being the product of stress is the first step towards emotional well-being.

Stage 1

- Do you have a sense of injustice or resentment against people you don't know such as big lottery winners or acquaintances who seem to have a much better life than you?
- Do you say 'should', 'ought to', 'must' a lot?
- Are minor niggles with neighbours or colleagues dominating your thinking?

Stage 2

- Do you feel guilty about being unhappy with your life?
- Do you find it hard to motivate yourself?
- Do you feel tired all the time?
- Do you lack confidence and self-esteem?

Stage 3

- Have you had repeated problems for a prolonged period of time?
- Do you have trouble remembering the last time you really laughed out loud?
- Are the people around you a constant source of disappointment?
- Do you think that life could be so much better if you could only resolve one negative issue?
- Do you suffer from constant anxiety?
- Do you think it is impossible to improve your situation?

If you ticked any statements in stage 1, you'll benefit from finding more pleasure in the life you've got – seeking out good feelings will make a huge difference to your state of mind.

If you ticked any in stage 2, stress is having a serious effect on your mood and could be pushing you into depression. Read on, but consider talking to your doctor.

If you ticked any in stage 3 it's time to consult your doctor. You might benefit from counselling.

When repetitive thought patterns or overwhelming anxiety are making life miserable, you might want to consider cognitive behavioural therapy which is designed to work in a matter of weeks.

Why not get started by trying this...
Lemon balm helps beat anxiety and irritability.
You can buy lemon balm in supplement form at your chemist or find a supplier on the web.

Key 32
Deal with the energy black holes

All around you are energy black holes, people who are unhappy, negative or angry and who would like nothing more than to drag you into their stressful world. And there is absolutely nothing you can do about them.

The only thing you can change is your attitude. (There is a proviso to this – if your life is littered with difficult people out to get you, then with respect I might suggest that it's got something to do with your expectations.) But sometimes, even most times, it's not you – it's them.

Some black holes are strangers

Other people have their own agenda. You can't know what it is and you can't change it. Take a tip from Rosamond Richardson, author and yoga teacher. She recommends visualising yourself surrounded by white light, creating a protective bubble around you. Negativity just bounces off this white light and can't affect you. Sounds nuts, but it works. Try it and see.

Some of them you share a life, a home, a bed with...

Don't waste a moment dwelling on how much less stressful life would be if only John would be kinder, Mum would cheer up a bit, Emily was more help around the home, or your boss was less aggressive.

This is a surprisingly telling little exercise that you can do in five minutes on the back of a napkin. It may give you a shock. Make a list of the people with whom you have regular contact. Then divide that list into three categories:

■ The energisers: They look after you in every way. They give great advice. They bring happiness to your life.

■ The neutrals: They're OK. Neither a great help nor a drain.

■ The drainers: They're users, people who don't deliver, let you down and bring you down. They also include gossips, people whose conversation is sexist or racist and the bitchy, sarcastic types whose conversation, no matter how entertaining, makes you feel bad about yourself afterwards.

And you know what I'm going to say. Maximise time with the energisers. Look for them when you enter a room and gravitate towards them whether you've been introduced or not. We all know these people when we meet them. If you have too many neutrals, think how you can bring more energisers into your life.

And the drainers? Your time with them should be strictly limited. And if some of them are your closest friends, your family, your lover, you need to think about that very closely. You may feel unable to cut them out now (although that is an option) but you can limit the time for which they are allowed to suck you into their world.

Key 33
Take control

Don't let your working day be hijacked by others. The secret is to have your goals clear in your mind. Think weekly, then daily.

Don't be a slave to a daily to-do list. See the big picture. On Monday morning lose the sinking 'I've got so much to do' sensation. Instead, think 'What are my goals for this week?' Decide what you want to have done by Friday and then break each goal into smaller tasks that have to be undertaken to achieve all you want by Friday. Slot these tasks in throughout your week. This helps you prioritise so that the tricky and difficult things, or tasks that depend on other people's input, don't sink to the back of your consciousness. It also means you are giving attention to all that you have to do and not spending too much time on one task at the beginning of the week. Concentrate on three or four items on your to-do list at once so you don't feel overwhelmed.

Work with your energy cycles

Some of us operate better in the morning, some in the late afternoon. If your job demands creativity, block out your most creative periods so that you can concentrate on your projects. Don't allow them to be impinged upon by meetings and phone calls that could be done anytime.

■ Make the phone call you're dreading right now, otherwise the dread will sap your energy all day. Just get it out of the way.

■ Have meetings in the morning when people are frisky and they want to whizz through stuff and get on with their day. Morning meetings go much faster than those scheduled in the afternoon.

■ Check emails three times a day, first thing in the morning, just after lunch and just before you leave are ideal times. Keeping to this discipline means that you don't use email as a distraction.

■ Limit phone calls, talk to other people when it suits you, not them. In my working life I receive around twenty phone calls a day. Answer machines don't help me personally – the call-back list is another chore. This is how I turned it around. The most time-effective way of using the phone is to limit your calls as you do your emails – to three times a day. Make a list of calls you have to make that day. Call first thing. If someone isn't there, leave a message and unless you have to talk to them urgently, ask them to call you back during your next phone period, such as just before lunch. That means neither of you will linger over the call. Your other phone time should be around 4.30 p.m. for the same reason. Of course, you can't limit phone calls completely to these times but most of us have some control over incoming calls.

Why not get started by trying this…
Create a 'virtual you' if you're getting stressed out in the office by the demands of others. When you're an administrative lynchpin, set up a shared file where people can go to find the information or resources they'd usually get from you.

Key 34
Never procrastinate again

Procrastination is stress's best friend. It's not big, it's not clever but for most of us, it's a way of life. But no longer! Here is the best method for overcoming it, here's how to get straight to the point, no beating about the bush or going round the houses. It's Mark Foster's rotation method from his brilliant book *Get Everything Done*.

You need pen, paper and a watch but a kitchen timer with a bell works best.

1. First make a list of your tasks. (Here is my list for this morning: write two ideas for this book, organise dinner party, do washing, make phone calls to pay some bills.)

2. Against each item write 10, 20, 30. These represent blocks of minutes that you are going to spend on each item in turn. So my list would look like this:

   Write book 10, 20, 30
   Organise party 10, 20, 30
   Laundry 10, 20, 30
   Pay bills 10, 20, 30

3. Start with the task that puts you off least. Set the timer for 10 minutes. Do the task for 10 minutes. (I have my load of laundry on comfortably within the 10 minutes.)

4. When the timer rings, *stop*. Wherever you are in the task. *Stop*. Score through the 10 next to the task.

5. Set the timer for 10 minutes. Start the next task. (It takes me the whole 10 minutes to get the paraphernalia together to pay the bills. Note: I'm no longer resentful about paying the bills, I'm irritated that I can't get on with it.)

6. Score through the 10 on the list and start the next task. (Writing. The task that is most formidable, but buoyed on by the fact that I've made a start on the mundane tasks, I sit down, make some notes and start typing. The timer rings mid-sentence. Note: I'm disappointed that I have to leave my task and move on.)

7. Score off 10 and start next task. (I look through recipe books for 10 minutes and add some names to the invitation list for my dinner party.)

8. Score off 10 minutes. Now move on to the first task again but set the timer for 20 minutes. Repeat the entire process. (The next load of laundry takes 10 minutes but I score off the 20 next to laundry as there's nothing more I can do. I set the timer to 20 minutes for the bills. I am halfway through paying the last bill when the timer goes. Score off 20. I move back to the writing with a sense of relief – that's the job that's most important and because of my 10-minute start I'm raring to go. When the timer goes after 20 minutes, I go back to the party, finalise the guest list and decide on the menu. Back to the laundry – 30 minutes. This takes much less than 30 minutes. Now I go back to my computer and complete another 30 minutes. After 30 minutes I pause and look at my list. All the chores have been completed. I'm where I want to be – sitting at my computer and enjoying

writing, so I set my timer for 40 minutes and carry on, promising myself a cup of tea at the end. I'm so into it after 40 minutes that I bring the cup of tea back to my desk and carry on until lunch time.

This method works. I promise.

Why not get started by trying this…
Scan your diary for big projects coming up. Tomorrow spend just ten minutes working on each project. By giving a tiny amount of focused attention regularly to projects, well in advance, you accomplish them without even noticing.

Key 35
Be like Tigger – learn to bounce

Everyone gets stressed. Everyone gets disappointed. But how come some people are better at dealing with it than others? The answer is that they're natural bouncers, but you don't have to be born that way.

Disappointment does one of two things: it makes you bouncy (resilient) or it makes you bitter – and which way you end up is a more telling predictor of future happiness than rich or poor, nice or nasty.

Bounceability is easy in your twenties. Underneath the veneer of sophistication most twenty-somethings are teenagers at heart convinced that their life is going to be fabulous. But during our thirties, the decisions we make pretty well determine what sort of person we're going to be, and how we decide to deal with setbacks is one of the greatest determinants.

Each of us is born, apparently, with a happiness set-point which is genetically influenced, but crucially, not fixed. We can come from a long line of grumpy bastards but at the end of the day our genes only seem to account for about half of our propensity for happiness – or unhappiness, depending on how you look at it. However, what we learn from grumpy parents is likely to be a lot more influential than what we inherit. We learn that life is fixed, that we can't change, that we're not in control. But that's wrong. The thing to remember is this: your brain chemistry is not fixed. You can change it.

How? When bad stuff happens, ask yourself what are known as "coping" questions which challenge inflexible thinking. What would be useful for me to do right now? What is the reality, and what is merely my fantasy about this situation? Can I salvage anything from this?

Then ask yourself some 'serendipity' questions. Why is it good that this is happening? What am I learning from this? What could I do to turn this situation around?

Ultimately, what it comes down to is remembering that everything changes and change itself is the source of stress. Bad stuff happens to good people. But there are plenty of people who have had every disappointment in the book and still lived useful, happy lives. And before you mutter 'bully for them', science will tell you that there's no reason why you can't be one of the bouncers too.

Key 36
Make space by de-cluttering

Get rid of your clutter and you're free to redefine yourself. Life becomes a lot simpler.

I started de-cluttering about ten years ago, and I haven't stopped since. It's addictive, it's life affirming. Nothing makes you feel so serene and in control of your life as chucking out stuff you don't need.

Chuck it out, lose the guilt

How does it work? Most of us live among piles of ancient magazines, defunct utensils, clothes that neither fit nor suit us. The Chinese believe that all these unlovely, unwanted things lying about haphazardly block the flow of energy – the chi – in our homes. My theory is that by losing them, we lose a ton of guilt – guilt that we'll never fit into those hellishly expensive designer jeans again, guilt that we spent all that money on skis when we only go skiing once a decade, guilt that we never cook those fabulous dinners in those two dozen cookbooks. You get my point. Just about everything in your home probably engenders some sort of guilt. Cut your belongings by 90% and you do the same to your guilt.

The big clear up

'Useful or beautiful, useful or beautiful' is the mantra. If any single object doesn't fulfil one of these criteria, bin it. Cultivate ruthlessness. If you haven't worn it, used it or thought about it in a year, do you really need it?

Have three bin bags to hand as you work. One for stuff to chuck out, one for stuff to give to charity, one for things you want to clean or mend. Visit the charity shop as soon as you can – make it a priority. Give yourself two weeks to tackle the 'mend or clean' bag.

Something neither useful nor beautiful, but that you don't want to let go of for sentimental reasons? Put it away for a year. Time out of sight makes it easier to get rid of.

Do this little but often. Try a couple of one-hour sessions per week. I operate the forty/twenty rule: forty minutes graft followed by twenty minutes sitting around feeling virtuous. You get better at de-cluttering. Soon it's second nature. Do two to three sessions a month.

Find a home for everything you own. You're allowed one drawer that acts as a glory hole for all the odd items.

> ### Why not get started by trying this…
> *Try the 'one in, one out' rule. For instance, if you buy a new pair of shoes, then you must get rid of an existing pair. An added bonus is that this system protects you against impulse purchases of stuff you're not really fussed about as you have to focus your mind on what you'll chuck out when you get home.*

Key 37
Speed parenting is better than stressed parenting

Children pick up adult stress like a dry sponge soaks up water. When you're happy, they're happy. And when you're stressed? Yep, you got it. That's when you need focused parental skills. Calm parents usually means calm kids, but when you're frazzled, they reflect it and have a horrible tendency to get bad tempered, argumentative, clingy and sick.

That's because stress is contagious. You get stressed, your kids get tetchy – at best. At worst, they get ill. Most parents know the rule of 'reverse serendipity' that guarantees it's on the days when your car gets broken into and your job depends on you delivering a fabulous (and as yet unprepared) presentation that your youngest will throw a wobbly and hide under his bed refusing to go to school because he's dying.

It's not mere coincidence. Research shows that even when they're tiny, children pick up on their stressed parents' frowns, tense jaws, averted eyes and other physical signs of stress. In turn, they cry or become withdrawn.

Short-term answer

Explain that you're stressed out, tell them why, but also show them that you're working out a way to handle it. Your competence in the face of a stressful day is an invaluable lesson for later life.

Saying "I'm stressed, here's what I'm doing about it," and giving them a timescale of when they can expect you to be back to normal goes a long way towards reassuring them.

And on those days when it's all going pear-shaped, your kids are being unbearable and not letting you get on with what you have to do, then the best advice is to give them what they want – your time. This piece of advice was taught to me by a grandmother and I've been stunned at how well it works. Pleading for an hour of peace won't work, but ten minutes of concentrating on them – a quick game, a chat, a cuddle and a story – calms them down and they tend to wander off and let you alone.

Long term solution

More than all the myriad advice I've had on childcare from child behavioural experts, the most useful was from a taxi-driver who told me that since his three children were born he'd always made a point during the working week of spending ten minutes a day with each one of them. Ten minutes a day sounds meagre but it's enough – if you actually do it. It's better to be realistic and consistent than to aim for an hour and achieve it only once a week. Even worse is to keep interrupting your time together to take a call from the office. Chat, wash their dolly's hair, read a story (hint: older children still like being read to) – but treat that ten minutes as sacred.

> *Why not get started by trying this…*
> *Next time you talk to a child get on their level, eye to eye. They respond better. Kneel when they're toddlers. Stand on a stool when they're teenagers.*

Key 38
Get a kick out of life

When you're bored, dull, lacklustre, you're as stressed as it gets. And what you need is a bit more stress – the positive kind. Stress gives life piquancy and verve. Workers who aren't under enough stress are unhappier and unhealthier than those who have stressful, challenging jobs.

For challenge, read control. Because even though it seems a contradiction in terms, stressed people tend to have more control than they realise. And that sense of control is so delicious that most of us go out of our way to bring more stress into our lives, just so we can get the hit.

On the other hand, if your life is lacking in stress – or is quite challenging but you don't get any sense that you are in control – then you will be bored, frustrated and grim. You stop thinking you're a good person. You stop thinking you're successful. What they never tell you in all the reams about the evils of stress is that coping with it does wonders for your self-esteem.

Experts believe that our bodies are designed to be mentally and physically stimulated on a daily basis – whether it's running for the bus or meeting tight deadlines. When we put ourselves under stress, we are rewarded for it. When forced to perform, our bodies release adrenaline. This triggers feel-good chemicals such as serotonin, which flood our body as a reward for completing a difficult task. Resolving a problem gives us a hormonal buzz and we feel terrific.

If you're bored and fed up with life, you simply might not be stressed enough. It's good to feel that you're competent, striving, achieving. In fact, I'll go further, it's impossible to feel this way without an element of stress unless you're an enlightened Buddhist monk. So if religion isn't your bag, it's imperative to find out what is. You might get your kick from being a Master of the Universe and killing the competition, you might get it from saving a wood of ancient oaks. You might get it from supporting your family without selling your soul. These are the big things, but little ones work, too. There are two important things to do:

1. Recognise what gives you a kick and seek it out. Next time you feel down in the dumps, don't head for the pub or turn to the biscuit tin. Get busy and up your stress levels. Set yourself a goal to be achieved by bed time. Tidying your desk, cooking a perfect soufflé, making two calls you've been dreading.

2. Give yourself the space to enjoy the kick. After completing any challenge or stressful act, always, always, always switch off. Remember you should either be relaxed or stimulated – not both at once. If your body wants to rest after meeting a challenge and you are full of anxiety about what you could or should be doing next, 'then your body doesn't know whether it is relaxed and repairing or stimulated and solving,' says stress expert, Liz Tucker.

Why not get started by trying this...
Sit back and grin. You'll find a big smile sends the message to your brain to relax even when there's absolutely nothing funny happening.

Key 39
Time to retreat

Some time alone with your own thoughts is deeply relaxing.

This idea is about obliterating the low-grade noise pollution that is now the background for most of our lives. Stop for a moment and think just how much noise is generated in your home now compared to the home you grew up in. Televisions in every room. Telephones wherever you go. Music playing where it never played before (in the workplace, on the end of the phone while you wait).

This constant barrage of noise is stressful. Here is a three-step plan to give yourself a break:

1. Switch off the TV. Television will eat up your life. Some nine year olds are watching up to four hours a day and these children perform less well on all measures of intelligence and achievement. TV does exactly the same thing to adults. It is such a very passive form of entertainment – it's been proven that just lying on the couch doing nothing burns off more calories than watching TV, presumably because at least you're generating some thoughts in your head.
2. Be silent. This is difficult to manage if you live with other people. But take a day off work and experiment with no noise. No TV, no radio, no phone – switch them all off.
3. Retreat. The best way of doing this is to go on a dedicated retreat – all sorts of institutions, religious or otherwise, run them. You can retreat and do yoga or dance or write or paint – or do absolutely nothing.

Of course, you don't have to leave home for that. It's much easier if you can escape but it's not impossible to put aside the hassles of everyday life and retreat in your own home. Clear away any clutter. Put away laptops, phones, diaries, PDAs – all work paraphernalia should be banished. Make your house as calm, restful and serene as possible.

Seven steps to retreating

1. Set aside at least twenty-four hours, preferably longer. Warn everyone you know that you don't want to be disturbed.
2. If you have family, do the best you can to escape. One way of doing it is to come back on your own a day early from a break, or leave a day after everyone else.
3. Get in all the food you'll need. Plan ahead. Make it especially tasty and nutritious. You don't want to have to venture out for supplies.
4. Switch off the phone. Don't open your mail.
5. Don't speak.
6. This is your opportunity to go inwards and not only relax fully but work out what you really want to do with your life. For that reason keep the TV and radio off. Listen to music if you like but make it classical and not too emotional. Limit reading to an hour a day.
7. Write in a journal, paint or draw, invent recipes. Do anything creative.

Better yet, be very still. Lie on the couch with a blanket and your thoughts. Breathe. Stay silent for as long as you can.

Why not get started by trying this...
Listen to some Bach, Chopin or Beethoven prior to falling asleep. It's been shown that people who listen to classical music in bed fall asleep more easily and sleep better than people who watch TV or listen to other sorts of music.

Key 40
Too stressed to sleep?

Facts:
- The most reliable predictor of depression is insomnia.
- Sleeping less than six hours a night is linked to increased obesity.
- Sleeping less than seven hours a night is linked to increased mortality.

Depressed, fat, dead: you've got to sort this sleep thing out.

If you have trouble sleeping, it's worth reiterating that insomnia is like losing weight. It's not enough to know what to do, you also have to act on it. Chronic insomniacs often stay up half the night drinking tea or alcohol, smoking, watching movies. And then they go to bed and listen to the radio and read until finally around 4 a.m. they doze off. If you don't sleep well here are some key strategies:

- Don't drink caffeine for at least six hours before bed.
- Eschew alcohol and cigarettes for at least four hours before bedtime.
- Don't look at any sort of screen for three hours before bedtime.
- Get outside every day and do some exercise.

If this doesn't work...

Then the best advice is to think of yourself as a child. Infants are not born with the ability to soothe themselves to sleep, they need to learn it. You will have to re-learn the skill. You need consistency. A cast-iron routine that never wavers.

Stop all chores and any form of work at least two hours before bedtime. Develop a wind-down routine that starts about an hour before bed. Gentle yoga is brilliant for this, or you could lie on the sofa and listen to quiet music. Then run a hot bath. The bath is important. To counteract the heat your body lowers its temperature. Lowered body temperature triggers sleep. For that reason your bedroom and bed should verge on the cool. Cosy down in bed and read a book that isn't too thrilling and requires a little effort – Shakespeare's good, I find. Jane Austen is soothing. Do this every single night for a week.

If this doesn't work...

OK, let's get radical. You cannot sleep. You either can't get off to sleep or you wake early but you spend an inordinate amount of time tossing and turning. So don't. Just get up and do something else. See your insomnia as a gift. It's the chance to improve your life, to carve out some time for yourself. And before you dismiss this as utopian rubbish, a friend of mine recommended this tip to me, it had revolutionised her life within four months. She used to go to bed at 11 p.m., wake at 4-ish and then lay awake until the alarm went off at 7 a.m., feeling miserable. So she started setting the alarm for 4.30 and getting up then instead. After a few days she discovered her optimal time was 5.30 a.m. She'd have a cup of tea and plan her day. She'd do a little work

('Really impressed the clients when they got emails that I'd sent at 6.15'). A sleep expert advised her that sleeping only six hours a night wouldn't do her any harm at all if she managed a nap – humans are designed that way.

> *Why not get started by trying this...*
> *Try a 'power nap' for increased evening productivity. But if you're worried about feeling groggy when you wake, try drinking a strong coffee, then nap. It takes at least thirty minutes for the caffeine to kick in which gives you thirty minutes to doze.*

Key 41
Have a holiday at your desk

Imbue your working day with a certain grace and glamour and you'll be amazed by how much tension seeps out of your life. You'll be raising your standards and that means lowering your stress levels so you will relax. It takes a little thought. But you can have a holiday of the mind on even the most mundane day.

Reboot your commute

Give your journey to work an overhaul. Set yourself targets. Instead of a drag, see it as a purposeful part of your day. If it involves walking, buy a pedometer. Learn a language. Use the time to repeat your mantras for the day. Be creative: write a page of free-hand prose on the journey in. Start working up the characters for your novel. The list is endless.

Boost your environment

Your starter question: what five changes would make your work environment more pleasant? Here's my list:

1. Getting rid of piles of papers and magazines that need to be filed.
2. Investing in a china cup and no more sharing the office's grubby, chipped ones.
3. Cheering up my desk with a bunch of pink tulips.
4. Cleaning my keyboard – so filthy it's a health hazard.
5. Turning down the ringtone volume on my phone.

Find some way to make your surroundings more pleasant, every day.

Beat the mid-afternoon slump

When you feel the slump kicking in, stop working and get away from your workstation if you can. Go for a short walk in the sunshine, or take a nap. If you can't, try this: palm your eyes in your hand for a few minutes and visualise a calm and beautiful place. See this in as much detail as possible.

The journey home

This needs a different mood from the journey to work. If you listen to music, make it different from the tunes you play in the morning – slower, deeper. Small stuff like that really helps to emphasise that this is your transition period. Have a project that you work on at this time (planning your holiday is good). And if you read, keep the tone light. If in the morning you practise your French verbs or read the novels of Dostoyevsky, read P.G. Wodehouse on the way home.

Spread love

When you pass someone in distress send them 'serenity' or 'calm' as a thought. Spread good and happy thoughts wherever you go. Smile. Be gracious. Be kind, compassionate, a force for good.

Why not get started by trying this...
Clothes can play a huge part in improving the quality of our life. Every morning choose one thing that makes your heart sing – a colour you love, a fabric that embraces you, a piece of jewellery with sentimental attachment. Next time you're shopping buy clothes that help you radiate confidence.

Key 42
A five week plan to make life easy for yourself

Give up coffee, don't smoke, take exercise – we're always being told that unless we do, our stress levels will rise. Wouldn't it be great if it was all a big, fat lie?

I'd love to tell you that it was, but I can't. Without a doubt, one of the main reasons our bodies and minds are buckling under stress is that our lifestyles are about as far removed from relaxation as it's possible to be.

Try one of these suggestions for a week or so, and when it's second nature add another.

Week 1

Drink a glass of water with every meal and every time you visit the bathroom.

This is self-explanatory. Just do it. There are lots of smart alecks who will tell you we don't really need all that water. But water is almost unique in being a substance with no downside. It also gives you more energy.

Week 2

Swap one of your regular cups of caffeine for one healthy cuppa. Caffeine stimulates the adrenal glands to work overtime. It's been found that four to five cups of coffee a day raises stress levels by a third. Living on the adrenaline produced by tea, coffee, fizzy drinks and chocolate is just plain daft. I know. I did it for years. Redbush tea is brilliant. Unlike normal tea it is good for you – full of antioxidants but no caffeine. Unlike herbal tea, it tastes nice. Aim for no more than one caffeinated drink a day.

Week 3

Eat breakfast every single day. Studies show that people who eat breakfast are more productive – and slimmer, incidentally – than those who miss it. I am not a breakfast person but again for the good of my health I forced myself to start eating within the first hour of waking up. This produces a huge difference in my concentration. Now I wouldn't miss it because I know that the quality of my work is so much better.

Week 4

Every day eat:
- One orange – for vitamin C (or another helping of vitamin C-rich food).
- One helping of oats, fish, meat or eggs (for vitamin B, necessary for beating stress).
- One helping of broccoli or one helping of carrots – just brilliant for antioxidants.

At lunch eat:

- One small serving of good-quality carbohydrate. Too much and you'll feel dozy but one slice of wholegrain bread or a fist-sized portion of wholegrain pasta or rice will release the feel-good hormone serotonin.
- Two to three servings of reduced-fat dairy, which is rich in natural opiates called casomorphins (have one serving with your evening meal if you have trouble sleeping).

At dinner eat:

- One small portion of good-quality protein (releases tryptophan which helps serotonin release).

This won't supply all the nutrients you need but it's a good start and it specifically delivers the nutrients you need to stay stress free.

Week 5

Exercise. It is the single best thing you can do to reduce your stress levels and the best thing you can do for your health full-stop (with the exception of giving up smoking). Aerobic exercise (walking briskly, running, swimming) burns off excess stress hormones. Yoga lowers blood pressure in a matter of minutes, and after half an hour, stress levels have dropped dramatically.

Why not get started by trying this…
Start your day with porridge: the best stress–busting breakfast is a bowl of the stuff. It's even better if you can throw in some yogurt or milk (for their stress-reducing nutrients). Oats have been shown to keep stress levels lower throughout the day than other breakfasts and although muesli made with oats is good, cooking the oats as porridge works best.

Key 43
Why it's a good idea to get out of your head

Here's a way of handling stress that could improve your sex life too!

If you want to win the battle against stress, pay attention – to everything except what's going on in your head.

Hundreds of research studies prove that meditation reduces hypertension, cholesterol and a load of other markers of stress-induced illness. It gives more energy, a happier disposition and a better sex life.

I want to be a meditator. God knows, I've tried. Like Vienna and elasticated trousers it's something I'm looking forward to in my later years. In the meantime, I will use an idea that delivers much of the benefit without all the spiritual expectations, and is easy to bring into play whenever you need it. A sort of meditation-lite, if you like.

Mindfulness came out of the work of Jon Kabat-Zinn, a scientist who runs stress-reduction programmes at the University of Massachusetts Medical Centre. Kabat-Zinn wanted to find a way of teaching patients how to kick-start their own healing powers. Like meditation, mindfulness gives control by helping you to listen to your body.

Lie down (although you can do this sitting if it is more convenient). It helps at first to close your eyes. Become aware of your breathing. Don't force deep breaths but 'see' in your mind your breath entering through your nostrils and flooding your lungs. Listen to the sounds of your breath. Concentrate on nothing else. When your mind wanders, let these thoughts float away, imagine them as little white clouds and return to the breath.
(That's it.)

It's recommended you be mindful for forty-five minutes a day for best results. If you can manage just five minutes (which is all I fit in most days), you will find it helps immensely. This keeps you calm when things gets hairy and seems to work especially well for maintaining your sense of humour when life seems dire. It appears to have all sorts of health benefits too – aiding healing and lowering blood pressure.

The point of this is to make you more aware of the here and now. It is quite shocking when you realise how often your mind is occupied with running over what has happened in the past and fantasising about what might happen in the future (and fantasy is all it is: none of us can know what's going to happen). The here and now is a great place to be – because nearly always in the here and now you are absolutely fine. Mindfulness transports you away from fear and towards self-reliance and self-confidence. You can use it when you're brushing your teeth. You can use it when you're having sex. It will automatically make any activity more profound and you more calm.

With practice you will find yourself falling into the mindfulness state at odd times – making dinner, crossing the road, in the middle of a conversation with your bank. This is the best way of turning 'space' into 'useful experiences'.

Why not get started by trying this…

Make your morning shower a mini-meditation session through the power of mindfulness. Listen to the sound of the water, and feel the sensation of the water on your skin. Let thoughts float down the plughole, concentrate only on what your body can feel, see and hear.

Key 44
Stop acting on impulse

Focus, concentration, sticking to what you've started. That will cut your stress levels instantly.

Yes, yes, yes. But how?

Ever get to bed and remember the stuff that you didn't get round to and feel disappointed and frustrated? When that happens it's time to go back to basics and use this idea. It helps you finish what you start and makes you feel on top of your life.

1. Before you go to bed tonight, think of something you want to achieve tomorrow. Keep it really small and simple. It doesn't matter what it is, but you have to do it. Make it something restful – you're going to read a chapter of a favourite novel. Make it useful – you're going to clean the cutlery drawer. Make it worthy – you're going to take a multivitamin. Take this promise extremely seriously. Promise yourself you'll do it – and follow through. If you don't, no excuses. You've failed. But you're aiming too high. Make your next promise easier to achieve.

2. Make a promise to yourself every evening for a week. And follow through.

3. OK, now you're going to make a list of some tasks that you need to undertake but have been putting off. You will need seven, one for every day of the week. Some ideas: starting on your tax return; making a dental appointment; cancelling the

gym membership you never use; sorting out your wardrobe; cleaning out the inside of the car; tackling just one of the many piles on your desk; grooming the dog; making a start on cleaning out the garage.

4. Write these down and keep them by your bed. Each night for the next week, pick one and promise yourself you'll do it tomorrow.

5. Write another list. This time put on it things that are worrying you and driving you mad. Suggestions: discover if your pension plan will pay out enough for you to live on; write a letter to that friend you're upset with; paint the kitchen. Put on the list everything that is driving you nuts. Then pick one and break it down into manageable steps. Promise yourself to do the first of these steps tomorrow, and every day from now on, make a promise to take another step forward. Don't let impulse drive you off course.

This is an exercise in mental toughness. Making promises to yourself that you never keep brings you down and, over time, breaks your heart. But by breaking difficult tasks down into manageable chunks and building the strength of character to follow through and get them out the way, you take a huge step forward in reducing stress in your life.

Warning: don't make more than two or three promises a day. Keep it simple.

Why not get started by trying this…
Making a promise to yourself every night and keeping it the next day is the route to mental toughness. Every time you keep a promise to yourself, stick some loose change in a jar. It's a good visual record of your growing focus and strength – and, of course, you get to spend the cash at the end of it.

Part 4
Making it all happen

Key 45
Your action plan to prevent, reduce and deal with stress

So far we have distilled how to stress proof your business and your life down to the 44 Keys that will have the most profound impact.

In this final part we simplify things even further by giving you an action plan.

To prevent business stress

- Systemise your business (Key 1)
- Identify the 20% of your customers, prospects and markets that are most profitable, and focus on replicating them (Key 2)
- Use the to-do list spreadsheet idea (Key 3)
- Use 'monkey management' to prevent upwards delegation of work (Key 4)
- Produce trend and variance reports (Key 5)
- Benchmark your business against your industry (Key 5)
- Use a One Page Plan every month (Key 6)
- Carry out a detailed review of your credit collection policies and systems (Key 8)
- Create a plan for each of the eight profit drivers (Key 9)
- Compete on maximum value not lowest price (Key 10)
- Choose your magic price (Keys 11 and 12)
- Talk to your accountant about your advanced tax planning options (Keys 13 and 14)

- Check whether you can use a trust to pay less tax when getting money out of your business (Key 14)
- Check whether you can structure your expansion plans to effectively pay no tax on your expansion profits (Key 14)
- Check whether you can claim more tax credits (Key 14)
- Check whether you can get a quadruple tax saving by incorporating (Key 14)

To prevent money stress

- Produce and regularly update your personal balance sheet (Key 15)
- Assemble and work with a strong Wealth Team (Key 16)
- Consider alternatives to conventional pensions (Key 17)
- Have your business valued regularly – and treat it as a key part of your retirement plans (Key 17)
- Start making your business more valuable and saleable – talk to a corporate finance specialist (Key 17)
- Make the most of tax free investments such as ISAs (Key 17)
- Check whether you can legitimately shift income between you and other members of your household to reduce your total tax bills (Key 17)
- Check whether you can structure your next house purchase so that you do not have to pay Stamp Duty and Land Tax (Key 17)
- Check whether there are currently any specialist investment opportunities that earn you a sizeable profit if the investment goes well, and give you a tax refund that is larger than the amount you invested if the investment performs badly (Key 17)
- Re-arrange your mortgage so that it costs less and is paid off sooner (Key 18)

- Use a twenty-eight day list to help you spend less and save more (Key 19)
- Use a £5 a day plan to build up a £1 million nest egg (Key 20)
- Put Powers of Attorney in place for you and your loved ones (Key 21)
- Make sure that you, your parents and other loved ones have done suitable care fee and inheritance tax planning (Key 22)

To prevent other types of stress

- Stop striving for perfection – good enough is good enough (Key 26)
- Spend an hour a day doing the things YOU want to do (Key 27)
- Always ask yourself 'Is this the best use of my time right now?' (Key 28)
- Always under promise (Key 28)
- Learn to say no (Key 30)
- Spend more time with people who energise you, and less with people who drain you (Key 32)
- Work with your energy cycles (Key 33)
- Stop procrastinating (Key 34)
- De-clutter your home and office (Key 36)
- Have a holiday at your desk (Key 41)
- Plan better – and stop acting on impulse (Key 44)

To deal with stress

- Designate Saturday as 'family time', and Sunday afternoon as 'me time' (Key 24)
- Learn how to relax properly (Key 29)
- Exercise (Key 29)
- Learn how to bounce back from setbacks (Key 35)
- Do the things that give you a kick (Key 38)
- Take time to retreat (Key 39)
- Improve your sleeping habits (Key 40)
- Put the right food and drink in your body (Key 42)
- Meditate (Key 43)
- If it gets really bad, talk to a doctor (Key 31)

Index